To my wife, Pamela Yvonne (née Lines), who has
shared my life for over 66 years and who has tolerated
my many hours on the computer writing books.

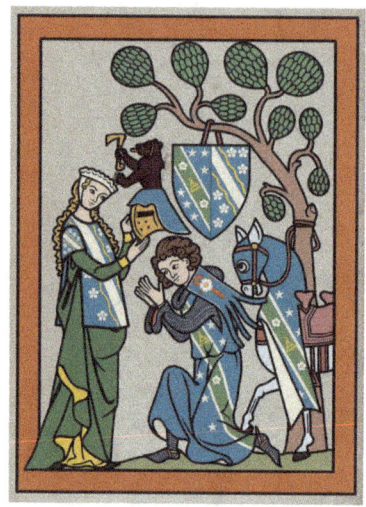

Dr the Chevalier Bernard Juby, K.LJ(J), SCrLJ, C.M.L.J.

Set in Book Antiqua

ISBN: 978-1-4457-2127-9

Contents

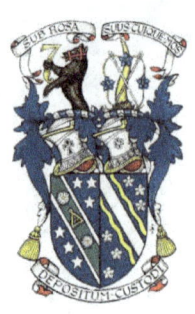

Introduction:

I first met Mr Thomas Walker (before he hyphenated Ferrers) when I was an Appointed Factory Doctor for Birmingham. I was the Vice-Chairman (Heraldry) of the Birmingham & Midland Society for Genealogy and Heraldry at that time – now Midland Ancesters (MA) - and he knew of my involvement.

He owned a factory in the North of Birmingham making chromed metal attachments for trousers and he gave me a set of colour slides (now lodged at the MA) of most of the heraldry at the manor.

He also invited me to visit the house and grounds to take further photographs. I combined the two to create a Power Point Presentation.

As a thank you I gave him some daffodil bulbs to plant in the grounds and which still give such pleasure to visitors each spring.

When the National Trust took over the property I wrote to the Curator with a copy of a room by room guide to the heraldry so that Guides would be able to explain them to any visitor who asked about them. He kindly sent me a set of floor plans and suggested that I changed the order slightly so that it matched the route taken through the house.

For anyone interested in the subject of Heraldry I would

thoroughly recommend, *"The Observer's Book of Heraldry"* by Charles Mackinnon of Dunakin & published by Warne. Although it is out of print second-hand copies are often available via eBay. It slips easily into the pocket and has everything a beginner needs to know.

A word of warning though - it can become very addictive!

Baddesley Clinton

Warwickshire

Compiled by Dr Bernard Juby, (Hon) F.H.S.

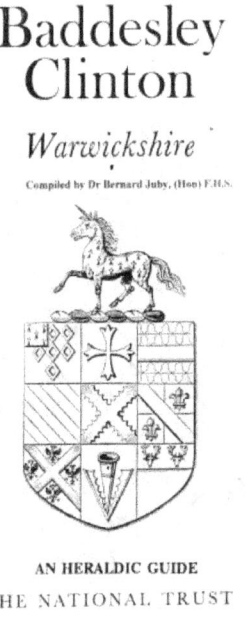

AN HERALDIC GUIDE

THE NATIONAL TRUST

Heraldry is all about colour and some 50 years ago colour printing was very expensive. On my flights to Brussells I regularly met publishers taking their manuscripts to Belgium where it was much cheaper.

As a result it was unillustrated but when I converted it into a PowerPoint lecture I added the colour photographs.

Many shields had been taken down from the Chapel and were in storage. They may still be there or now put on display? Similarly other heraldic artifacts may have been moved. They are referred to in the "Odds a Sods" section (pp. 48-49) - see if you can find them!

Dr Bernard Juby, Hon.FHS, etc.

A walk-through Guide to
The Moated Manor House

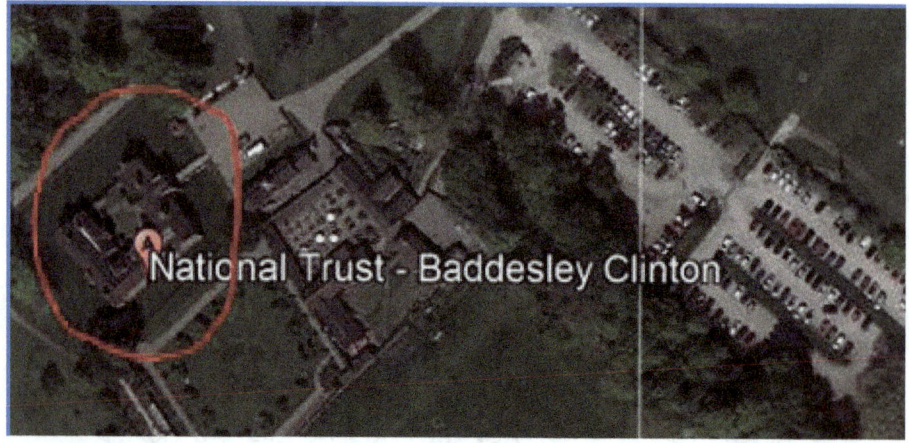

[Google Earth –
the large car park was not there when the photos. were taken.]

Baddesley Clinton,
Rising Lane,
Baddesley Clinton,
Warwickshire B93 0DQ.

+44 (0)1564783294

baddesleyclinton@nationaltrust.org.uk

We are fortunate that the Ferrers family had insufficient funds available to tear down the Hall in the 17th Century and cannibalise it to construct a Palladian Mansion - unlike Sir Edward Peto the Younger who destroyed the fine Elizabethan heraldic windows at Chesterton Hall c1656 when he re-built the Manor House. We thus have this Moated Manor be-jewelled with stained glass.

Let us go round the house, room by room and then go and visit the church.

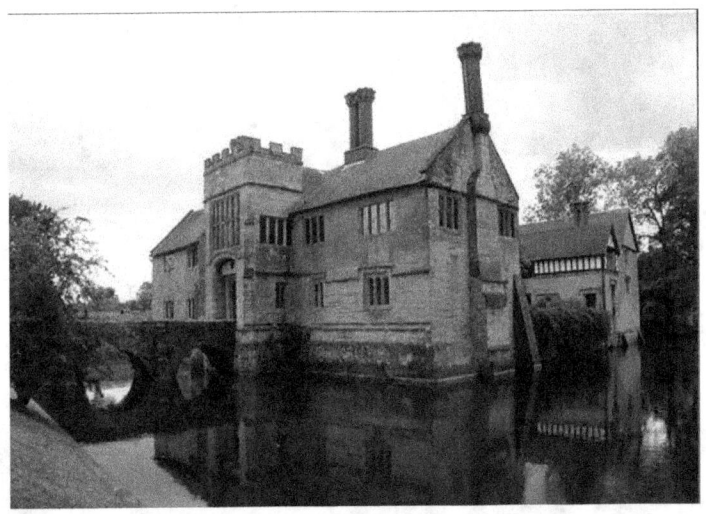

The Glass primarily commemorates the Ferrers family of which there were three branches.

Their pedigree shows the divergance in the 13th Century into Chartley and Groby, the further branching of Groby into Tamworth and Baddesley Clinton and the re-unification in the 18th Century when Harriett Anne Ferrers married Edward Ferrers of Baddesley Clinton.

(Some Peyto/Peto heraldry survives here in that Edward Ferrers married Anne Peyto long before Sir Edward Peto began his wrecking spree!)

From the large fore-court (with the Stable-block on the left) cross the moat and step inside.

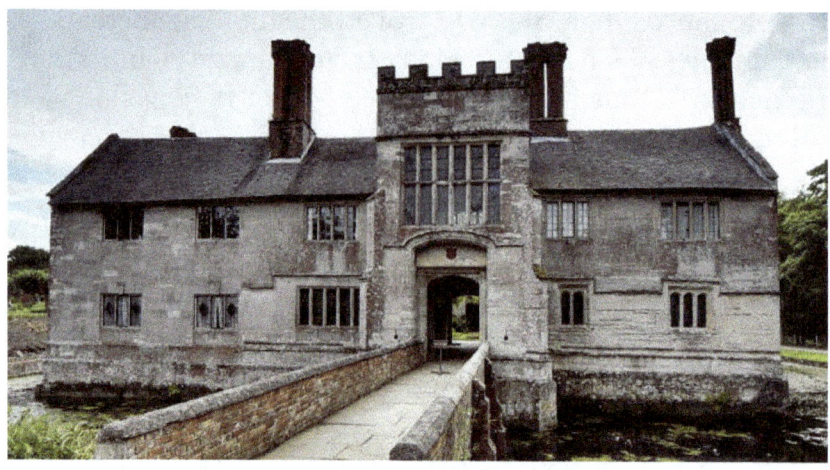

Notice the coat of arms over the archway - they are the arms of Ferrers of Groby (left) - it is surprising that they are not Ferrers of Baddesley Clinton (right):

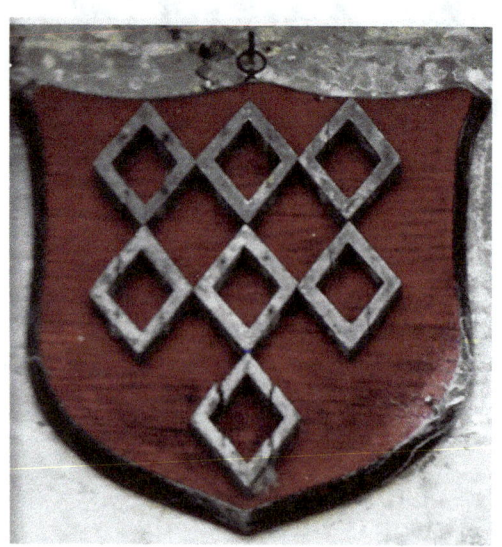

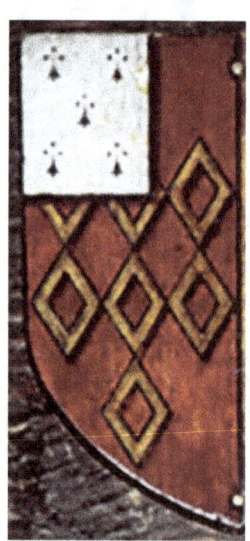

At certain times the de Quincy Arms are set out with flowers in the courtyard.

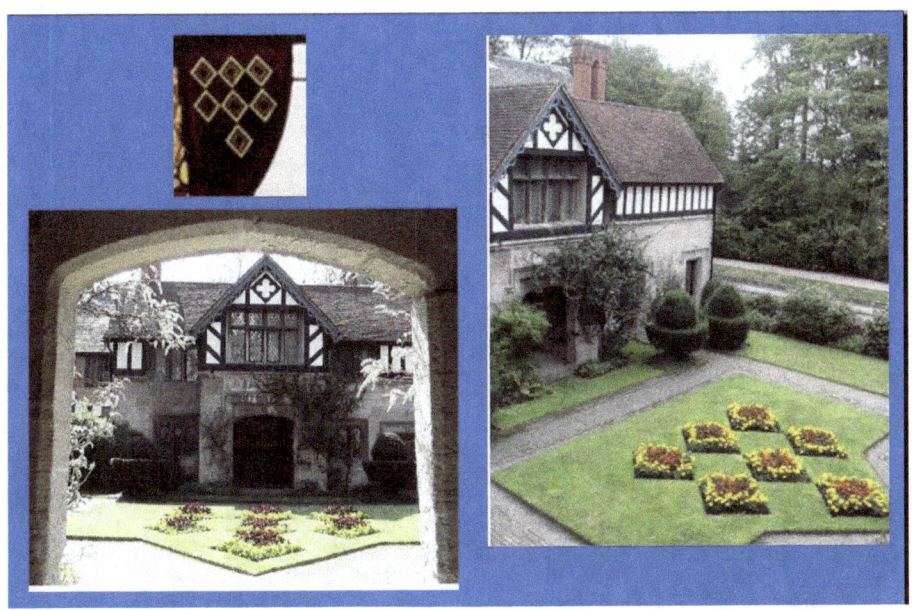

Entering the house to the Great Hall we first pass through the **Entrance Hall**

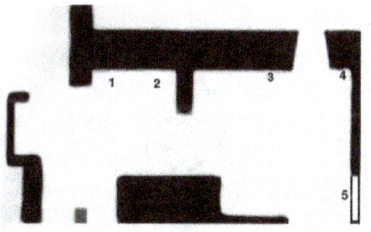

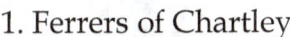

There are 2 shields
on the left-hand wall:

1. Ferrers of Chartley   and,   2. Ferrers of Groby

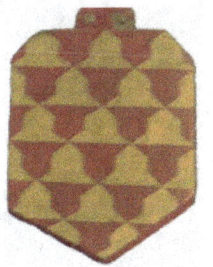

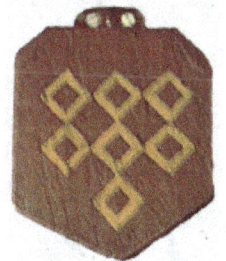

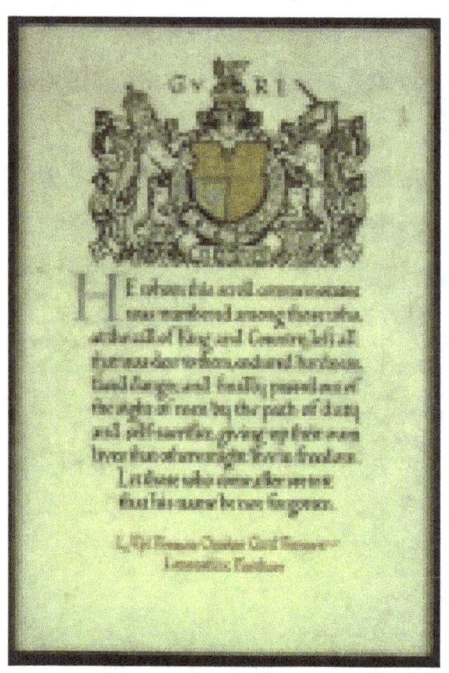

For Frances Charles Ferrers, born 1882 and married Muriel Hallimond.

A standard Citation given for all combattants killed in the Great War (1914-1918).

Left-hand Window 3:

For Henry, the eldest son of Sir Edward Ferrers of Baddesley Clinton impaling Catherine Hampden.

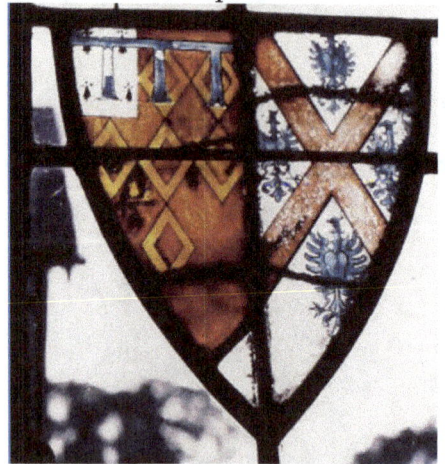

Right-hand Window 4:

For Henry Ferrers (the Antiquary) of Baddesley Clinton impaling Jane Whyte whom he married in 1582.

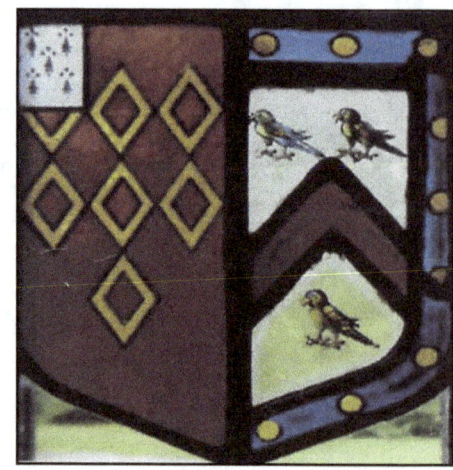

Above the Door 5:

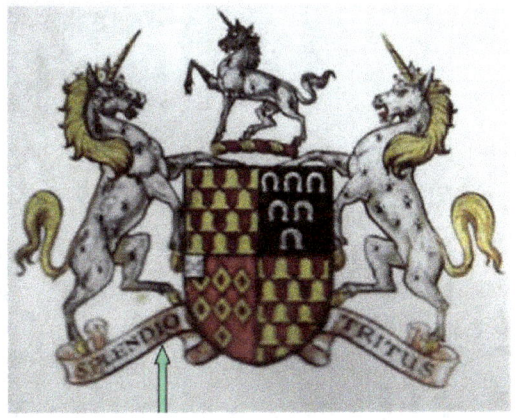

The 3 branches of the Ferrers' Arms:

Quarterly of 4:

1. & 4. Ferrers of Chartley,
2. Ferrers anc.,
3. Ferrers of Baddesley Clinton.

The Motto should read "SPLENDEO"!
c.f. the example in the Great Hall of Packwood House.

We now enter the Great Hall: -

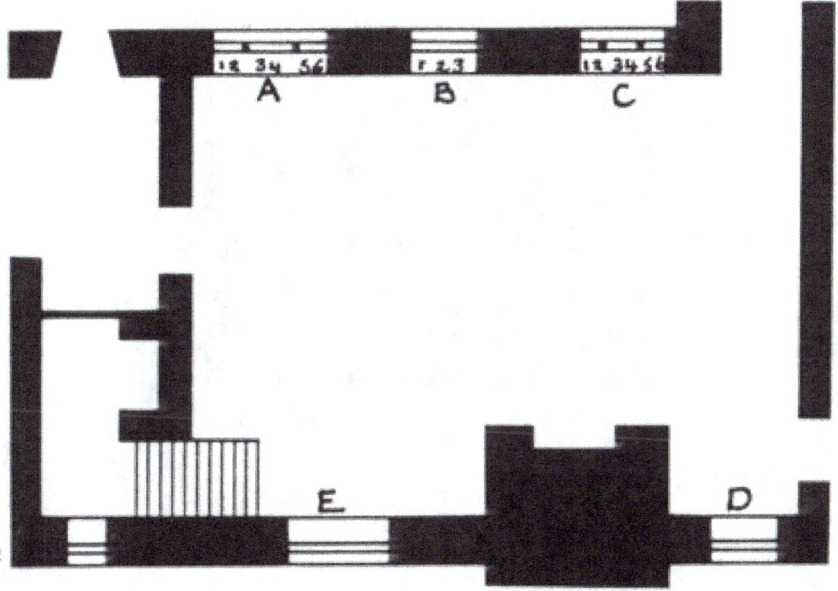

Clockwise from the left are,

Window A

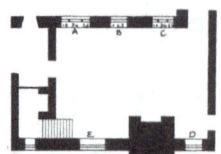

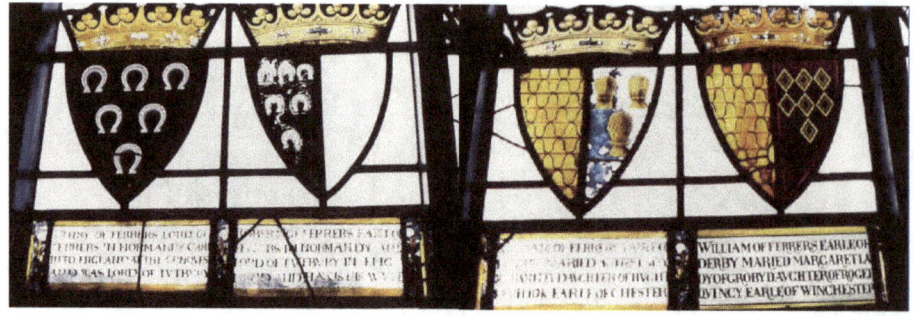

1. Ferrers Anc.
and
2. impaling ?de Vitry
For Henry, Lord Ferrers in
Normandy.

3. William de Ferrers of Chartley
m. the dau. of Ranulf, last Earl of
Chester.
4. William Ferrers of
Chartley m. Margaret, Lady of
Groby, dau. of Roger de Quincy,
Earl of Winchester.

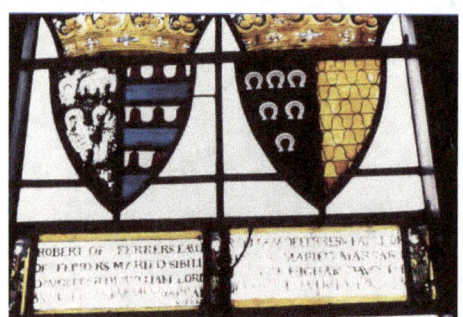

5. Robert Ferrers m. Sibill Braose
of Gower
6. Ferrers Anc imp. Ferrers of
Chartley (? for Margaret
Peverill).

Moving on to window B:

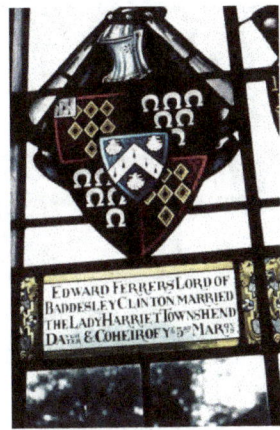

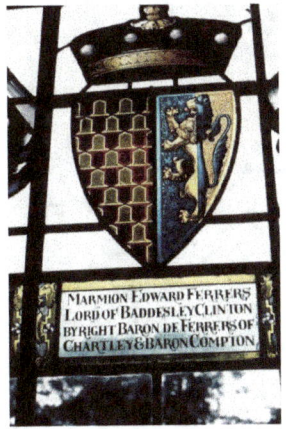

Ferrers of Baddesley Clinton quartering Ferrers Anc. with Townshend in pretence for Edward Ferrers and Margaret Townshend dau. and co-heir of the 3rd Marquis.

Marmion Edward Ferrers, Lord of Baddesley Clinton by right, of Chartley and Baron Compton impaling Orpen of Co. Cork

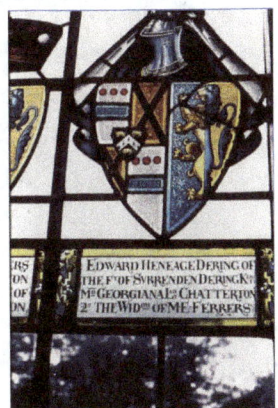

Edward Heneage Dering, son of Surrenden Dering
with Iremonger in pretence imp. Orpen
m.1. Georgiana, Lady Chatterton née Iremonger and
2. The widow of Marmion Edward Ferrers

Window C

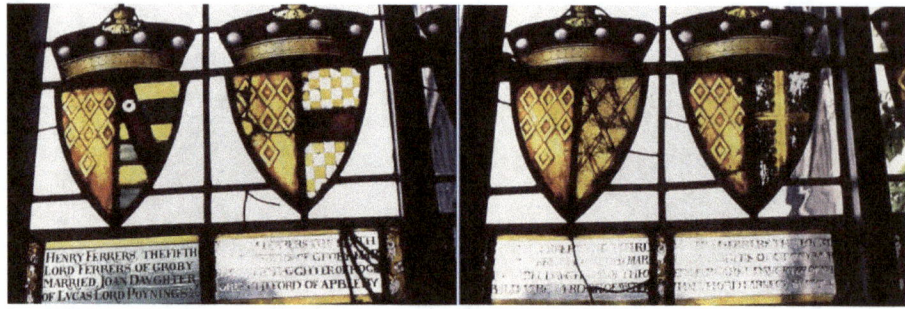

1. Henry Ferrers, 5th Lord Ferrers of Groby m. Joan dau. of Lucas, Lord Poynings
2. William Ferrers, 6th Lord Ferrers of Groby m. Philippa, d. of Lord Clifford of Appleby.

3. Henry, 3rd Lord Ferrers of Groby (d.1347) m. Isabel dau. of Theobald, Lord Verdon of Weble
4. William Ferrers, 4th Lord Ferrers of Groby (d.1372) m. Margaret dau. of William Ufford, Earl of Suffolk.

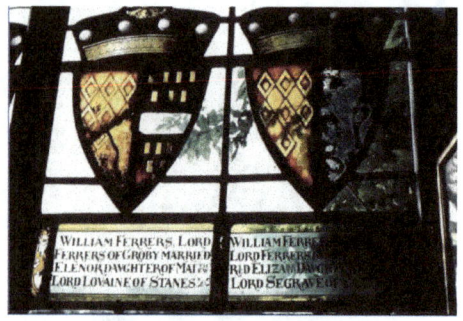

5. William, Lord Ferrers of Groby m. Elenor, dau. of ?Mathew, Lord Lovaine of Staines
6. William Ferrers of Groby m. Elizabeth, dau. of Lord Segrave ?Leicestershire.

Great Hall, South Wall Windows

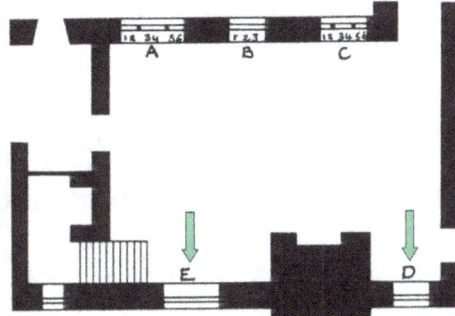

Both Windows D and E have 2 lights each. The fireplace is in between.

Window D, left-hand light

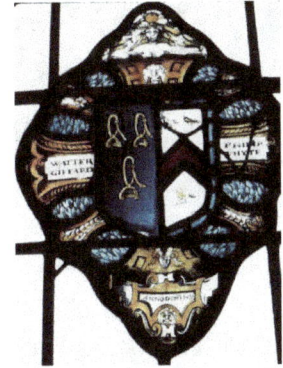

Walter Gifford impaling Philippa Whyte AD 1588

* Sir Henry Ferrers of Skellingthorpe, Lincs. was created Baronet in 1628. He m. Anne, dau. of James Scudamore. He d. 1663 and was succeeded by his son, Sir Henry Ferrers who died without heirs in 1675

Window D, right-hand

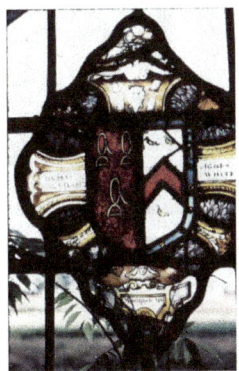

Thomas Scudamore, Co. Hereford
Impaling Agnes Whyte AD 1585 *

This tea caddy was on the ledge of Window C. It could still be there. It shows Dering with Iremonger in pretence:

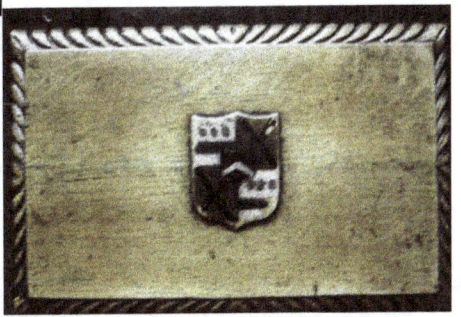

The Fireplace:

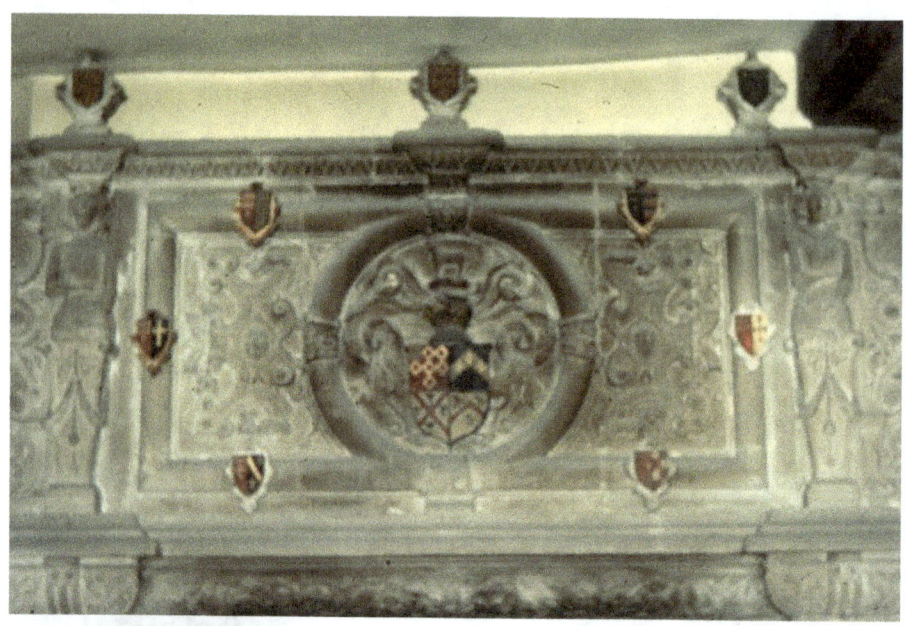

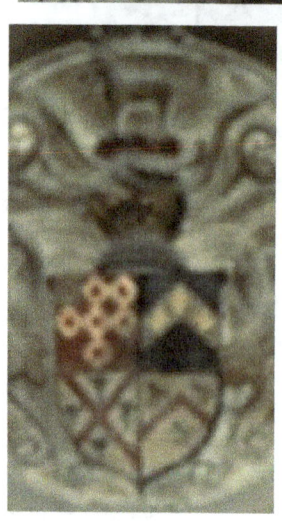

Centre:

Qtly. 1.Ferrers of Baddesley Clinton 2.Brome, 3,Hampden, 4, Whyte (Unicorn Crest).

This is surrounded by six impaled shields: (clockwise):

Ferrers anc./Braose: Ferrers of Groby/ Frevill: Ferrers of Groby/Heckstall: Ferrers of B. Clinton/Peyto (Edward, son of the Antiquary m. Anne Peyto 12th Feb. 1611): Ferrers of Groby/Verdon: Ferrers of Groby/Ufford.

Across the top on three filials are (l –r):

Ferrers of Chartley, Ferrers of Groby, Ferrers (Ancient).

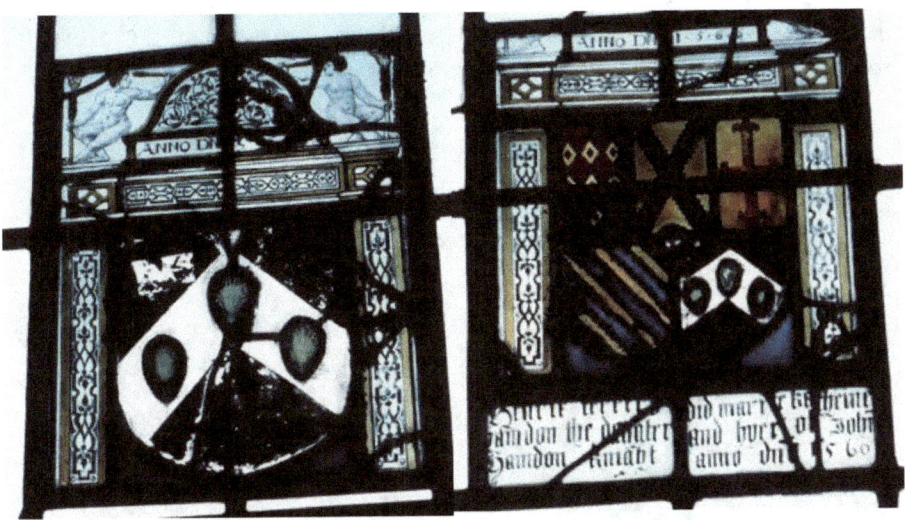

These are canting arms: The green on the chevron are leaves of broom.

Qtly. of 5 (3 and 2)
1. Ferrers of Groby
2. Botetourt
3. Frevill
4. Mountford
5. Brome
The inscription reads,
"Henry Ferrers did marrie Kathrine Hamden the dau. & hyer of John Hampdon Knight. AD 1560" (see Dining Room).

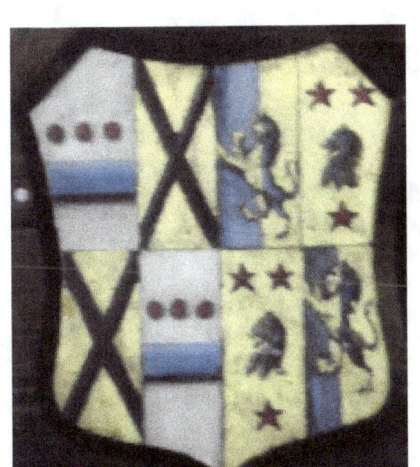

Over the staircase:
The quartered Arms of Dering impaling the quartered Arms of Orpen and Chatterton.
Edward Dering married Rebecca Ferrers (née Orpen) in 1885.

There are 9 wooden shields above the panelling which were placed there after the fire of 1940 destroyed the false ceiling. They are believed to be the work of Rebecca Dering. Old photographs also show that some of the window glass was reset in a different position.* The shield over the staircase was also by her.

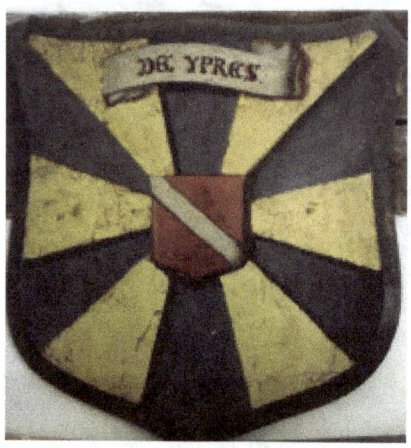

Bassiingbourne with Foliot in pretence.

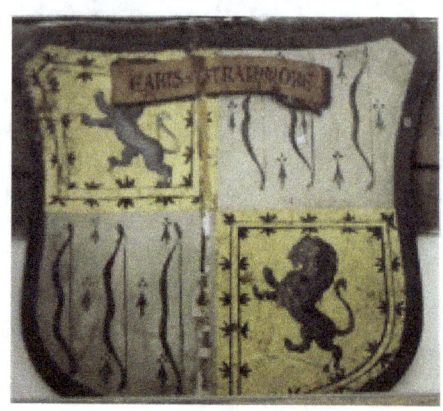

The canting Arms of Bowes-Lyon

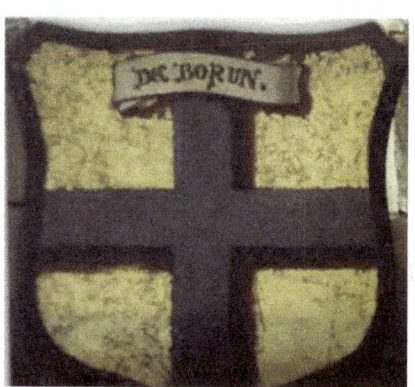

de Bohun

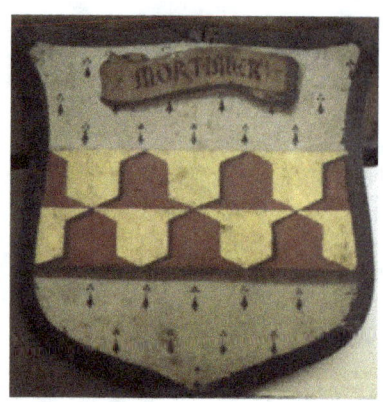

Mortimer

* See also *"Heraldry at Baddesley Clinton"* (an A4 guide to the heraldty) which contains much biographical information and a section on terms used in heraldry. It is currently out of print.

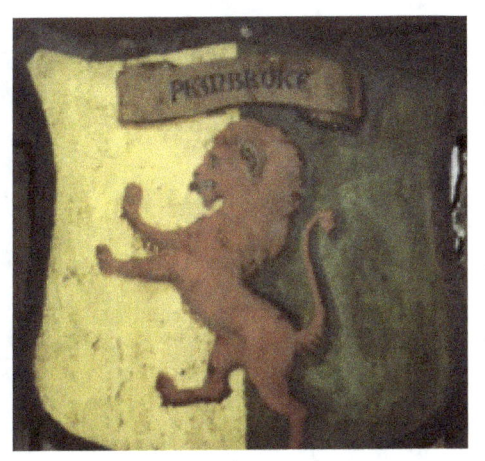

Pembroke

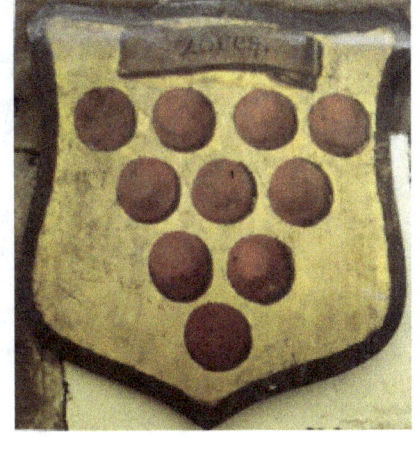

Zouch(e)

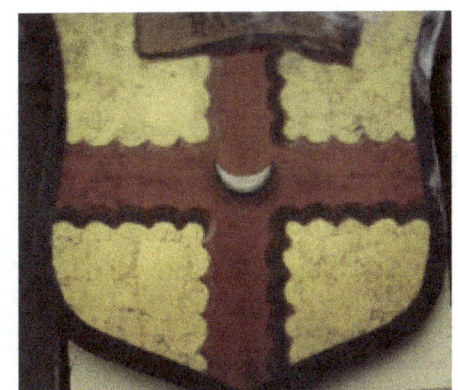

Hawis

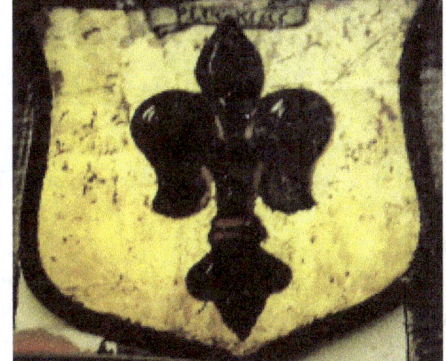

Pluckley

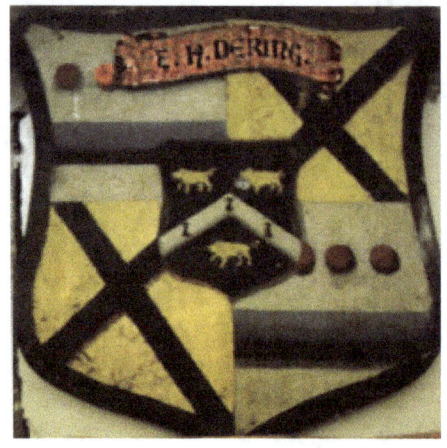

The quarterly Arms of Dering i & ii with Iremonger in pretence. Georgiana Iremonger was the widow of Sir William Chatterton who then married Edward Ferrers.

On the wall, between windows B & C are:

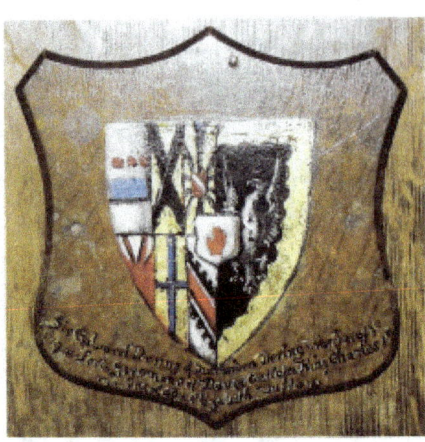

Sir Edward Dering impaling Tufton:
Quarterly of 6,
1 & 2 Dering i & ii,
3. Bassingborn with Foliot in pretence,
5. de Bohun,
6. Surrenden ("Argent a bend Gules cotised on the outer edge Sable.")
impaling Tufton.

and over the door from the Entrance Hall is:

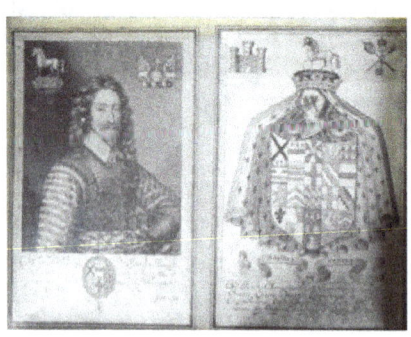

Although it is in black a white many of the quarterings are recognisable.

Rebecca Orpen married Marmion Edward Ferrers (1813-84) of Baddesley Clinton. She and her husband lived at Baddesley with her aunt, Lady Chatterton and her husband, Edward Heneage Dering. They became known as 'The Quartet', revelling in art, history and their religion. On the death of their spouses, Rebecca and Edward Dering were married.
Rebecca Orpen copied this print, dated 1640, but she added her own background & colour. The sitter was an ancestor of Edward Heneage Dering, Lord Warden of the Cinque Ports and Lieutenant of Dover Castle.

Over the door from the Entrance Hall are the Arms of Ferrers-Walker:

Quarterly of 4:
1. & 4. Walker (Granted by the College of Arms in 1940 when Thomas bought the Manor House from the Trustees.
2. & 3. Ferrers (Granted in 1941 when he changed his name)
"Gules 4 mascles conjoined 3 & 1 Or within an orle of the last."

c.f.the Arms of Groby..

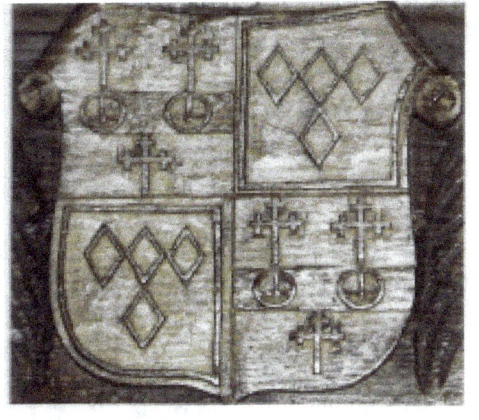

Below window D left are the carved Arlms of Ferrers of Groby. The four round buckles are also on the Ferrers-Walker Arms and are an allusion to his business.

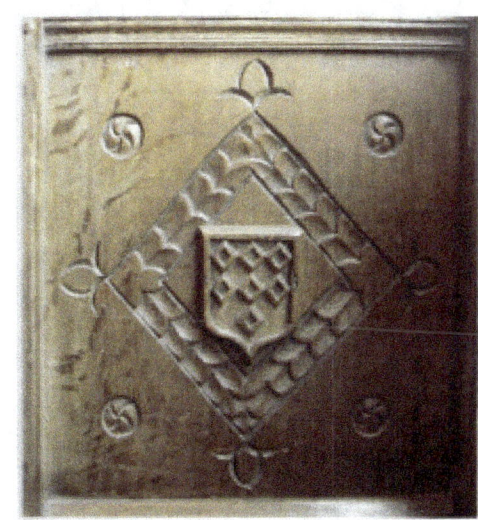

We now move into the **Drawing Room:**

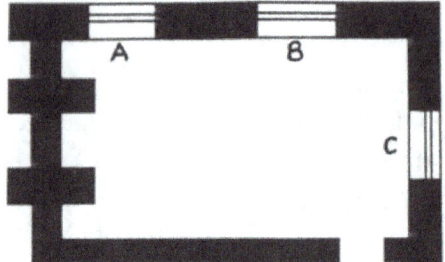

There are three windows each with two lights.

Window A - left-hand light: - right-hand light:

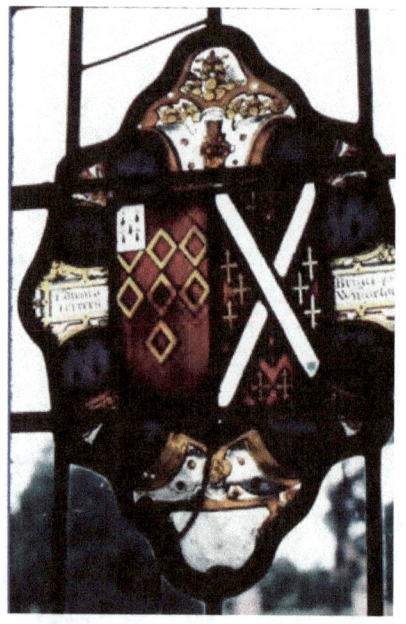

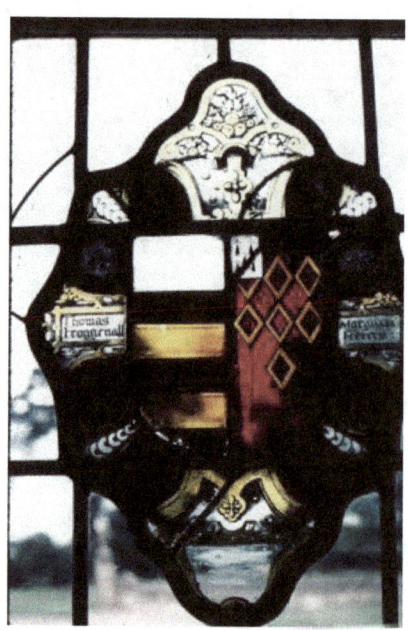

Ferrers of Badesley Clinton impaling Windsore (sic) for Edward Ferrers (b 1526) son of Henry (d 1564) who married Bridget dau. of William, Lord Windsor of Bradenham, Bucks.

Froggenhal impaling Ferrers of Baddesley Clinton for Thomas Froggenhall who married Margaret, dau. of Sir Thomas Ferrers d. 1535

Window B - left-hand light:

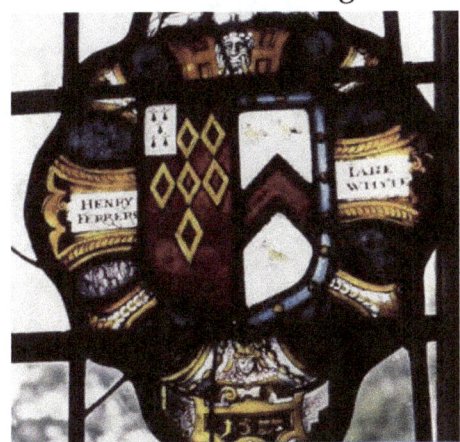

Ferrers imp. Whyte

For Henry Ferrers (1549-1633)
who m. Jayne, dau. of Henry,
son of Sir Thomas Whyte of
S.Wainborough, Hampshire.

- right-hand light:

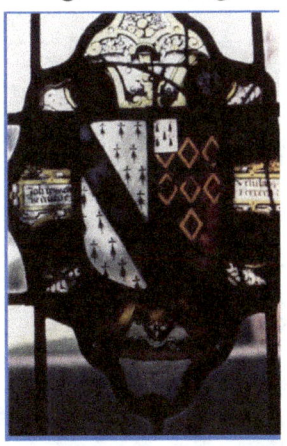

Beaufoy imp. Ferrers

For John Beaufoy, ward to
Sir Edward Ferrers (d.1535)
whose dau. Ursula he m.
c.1522)

Window C - left-hand light:

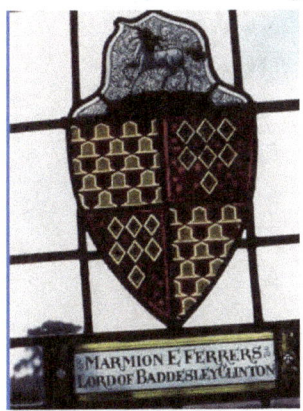

Chartley qtring. Groby

Crest is a Unicorn Ermine maned,
horned and tailed Or for Marmion
Edward, s. of Edward & Lady
Harriet Anne Ferrers Townshend,
eldest dau. of the 15th Baron Ferrers
of Chartley bringing together the last
of the lines of the two branches.

- right-hand light:

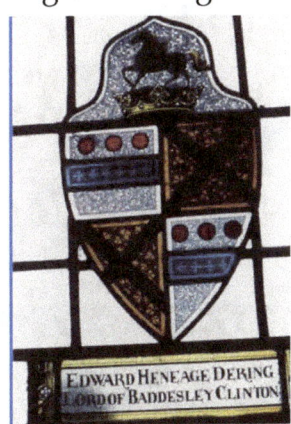

The Dering quarterly coat
(all diapered)

Edward Heneage Dering of
Surrenden Dereng, Pluckley, Kent
m. 1. Georgine Chatterton
?Iremonger and
2. Rebecca Dulcibella Ferrers, widow
of Marmion Edward

Overmantle:

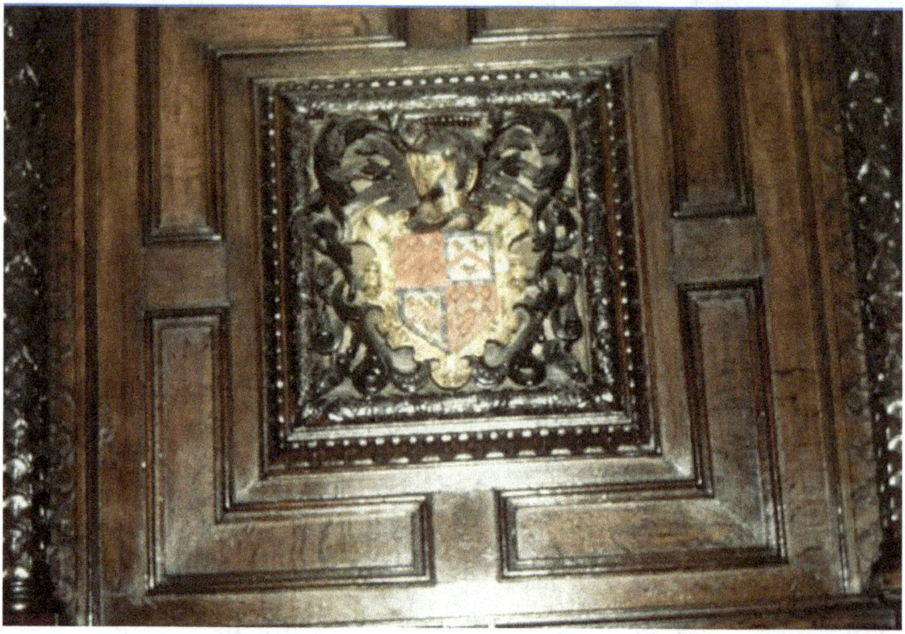

Ferrers of Groby quartering Whyte.
Jane Whyte married Henry Ferrers, the
Antiquary, in 1582.

We now move into the **Dining Room:**

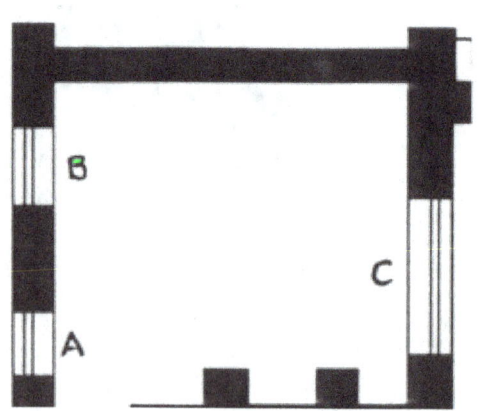

There are three
windows (the first
is clear), an
Overmantle and a
Court Cupboard.

Window B: Left

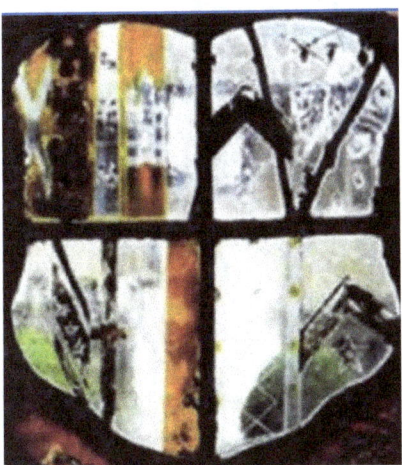

Centre

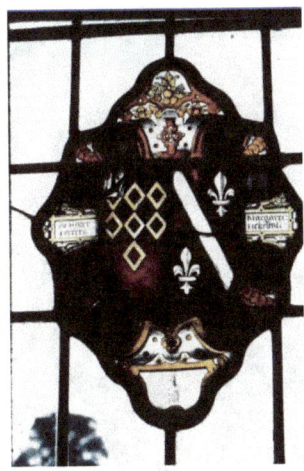

Windsor impaling Sambourne:
For William Lord of Bradenham,
impaling Margaret Sambourne.

Dexter - Qtly of 10
1. Windsor
2. Blount
3. de Ayala
4. Castile
5. Echingham
6. Beauchamp
7. Andrewes
9. Moleyns
10. de Byntworth

Sinister - qtly of 4
1&4. Samborne
2. Drew
3. Luddel or Lushill

Ferrers imp. Heckstall
for Sir Henry Ferrers who
m. Margaret, dau. and co-
heiress of William Hekstall
(sic) of Hekstall, Esquier
(sic).

Right)

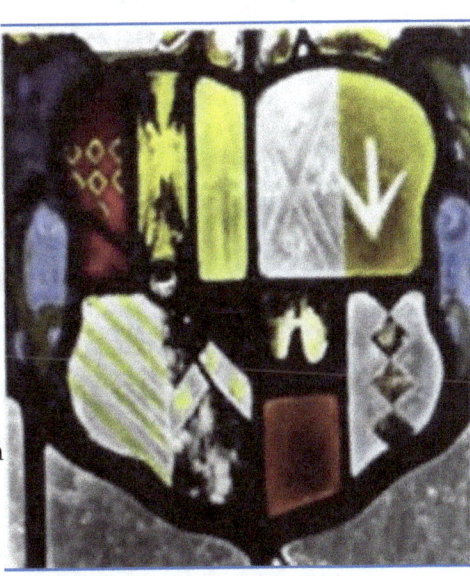

Probably for Henry Ferrers and
his wife Catherine Hampden:
 Qtly of 5
1. Ferrers of Groby
2. Botetort
3. Frevil
4. Mountford
5. Brome

impaling:
 Qtly of 4
1. Hampden
2. Sydney
3. Popham
4. ? Daniel (Staffs.)

Window C – 3 impaled coats,
Left: **Centre:**

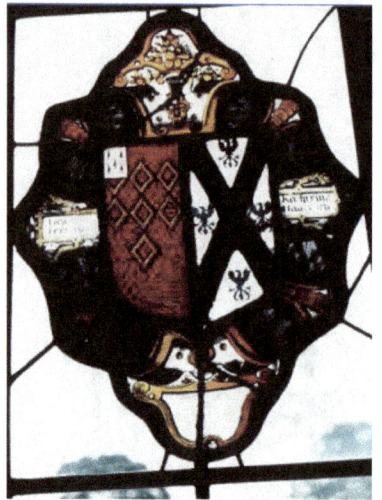

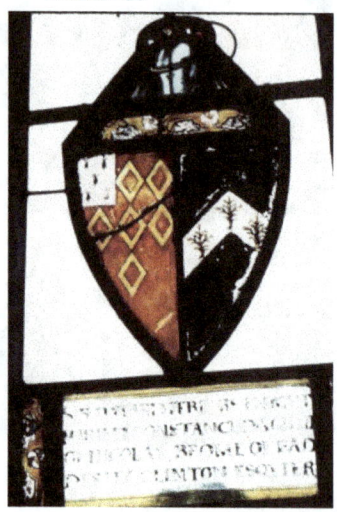

Ferrers impaling Hampden
for Henry Ferrers who
m. Kathleen Hampden of
Great Hampden, Bucks.

Ferrers impaling Brome
for Sir Edward Ferrers who
m. Constance, dau. of
Nicholas Brome of
Baddesley Clinton Esq.

Right:

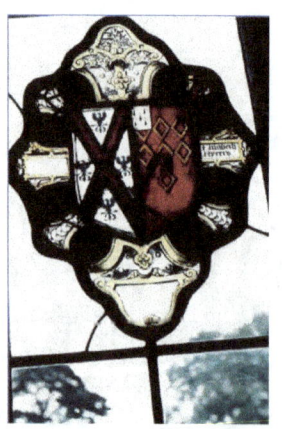

We now go upstairs -

Hampden impaling Ferrers
for Henrie (sic) Hampden who m.
Elizabeth Ferrers, dau. of Sir
Edward (who died 1535)

The Staircase:

Landing window, upper centre light

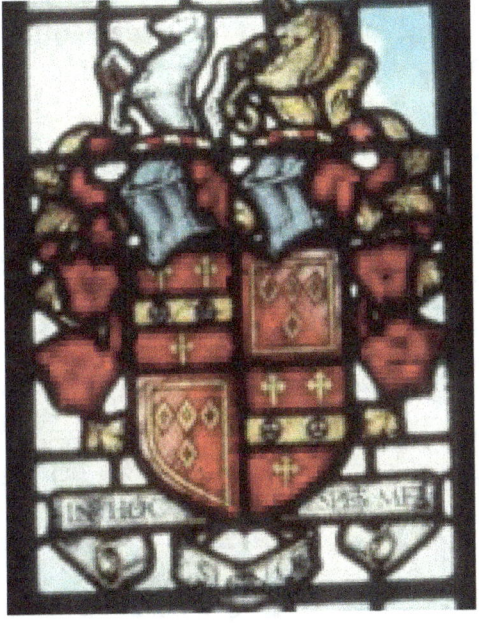

The Ferrers Walker qtd coat (also on the Stable Block) The inscription states,
"Thomas Ferrers Lord of Baddesley Clinton."

- lower;

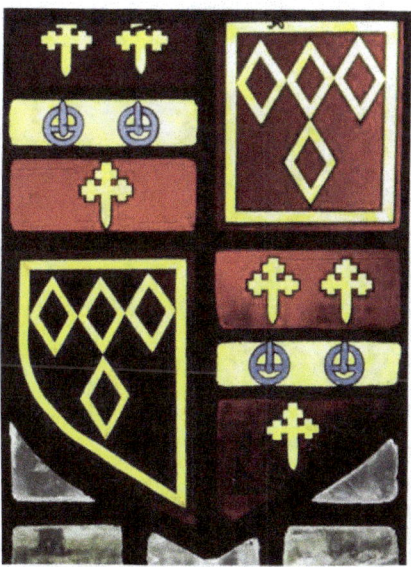

A similar s.g.w. commissioned by Thomas after the death of his father, with the inscription,
"Thomas Weaving Ferrers-Walker Protector of Baddesley Clinton."

We now go into **Henry Ferrers' Bedroom**

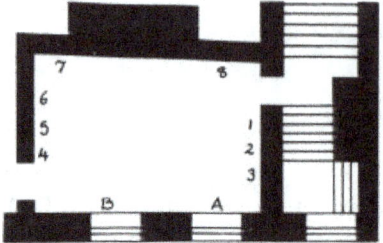

There are two heraldic windows, A and B, a carved oak overmantle and a frieze above the panelling showing 8 wooden shields.

Window A - left hand pane:

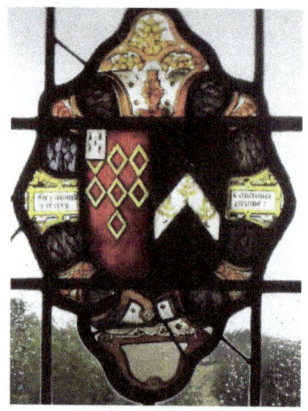

- right-hand pane:

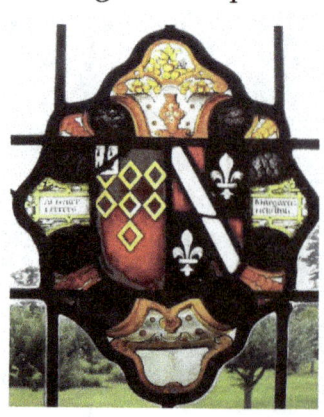

Left: Sir Edward Ferrers of BC impaling Constance Brome.

Right: Sir Henry Ferrers of B.C. impaling Margaret Heckstall.

Window B - left-hand pane:

- right-hand pane:

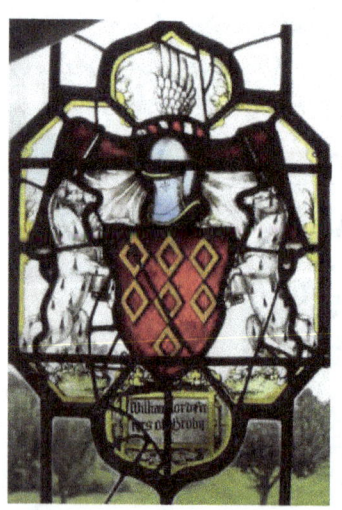

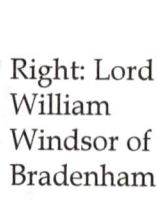

Left: Ferrers of Groby.

Right: Lord William Windsor of Bradenham

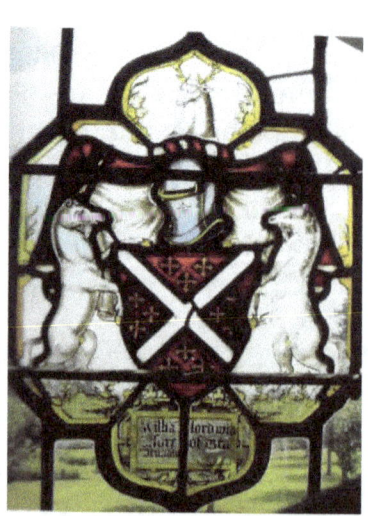

The Fireplace has an overmantle flanked by 2 shields:

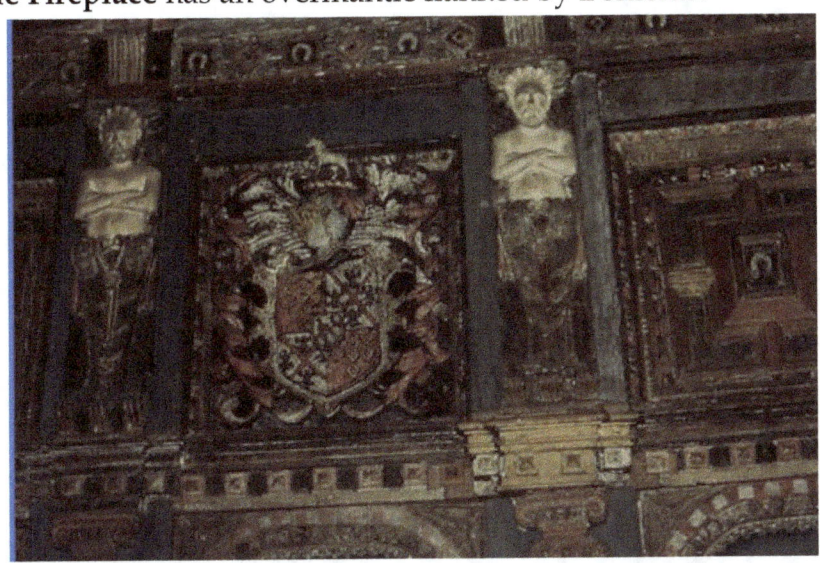

Groby quartering Hampden with Whyte in pretence.
The crest is a unicorn Erm. Note the horse-shoe badges and in
the spandrils of the arch beneath are Groby and Whyte.

The central
Arms enlarged:

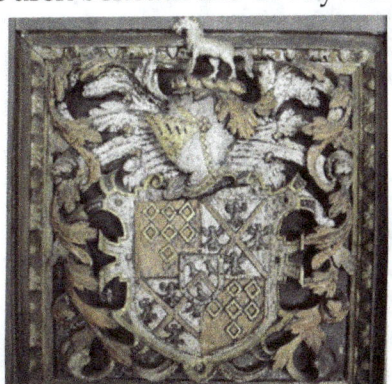

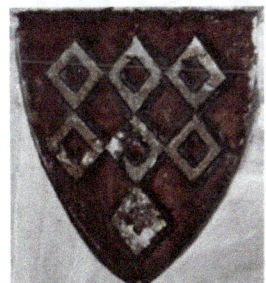

Left: Henry Ferrers of
Groby
("The Antiquary")

Right: Jane Whyte

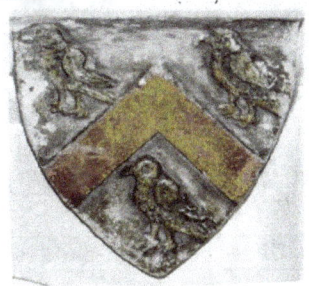

There are 8 painted shields around the panelling - one of which has been painted directly onto a panel:

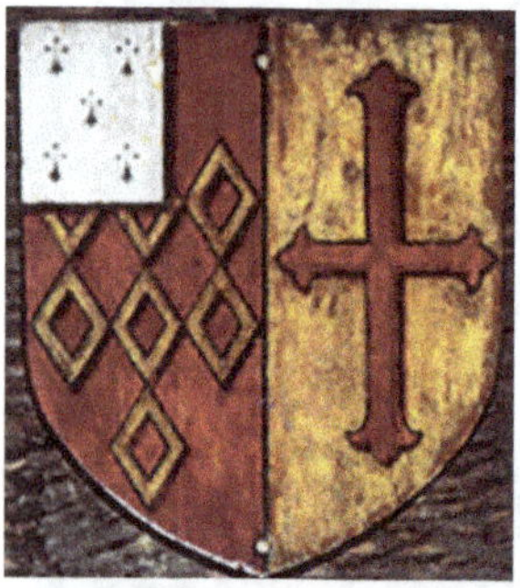

BC* imp. Frevill 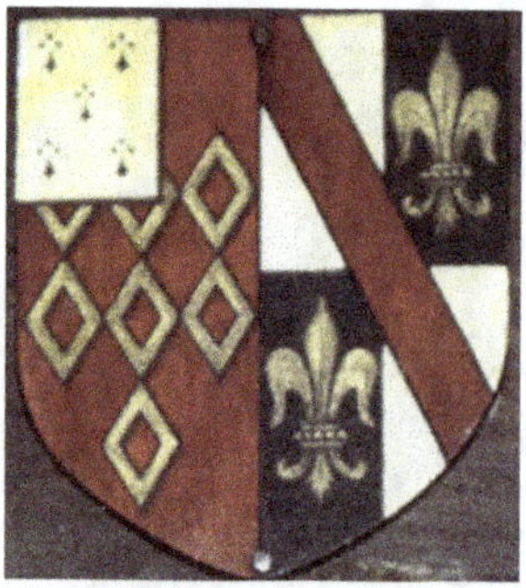   BC imp. Heckstall 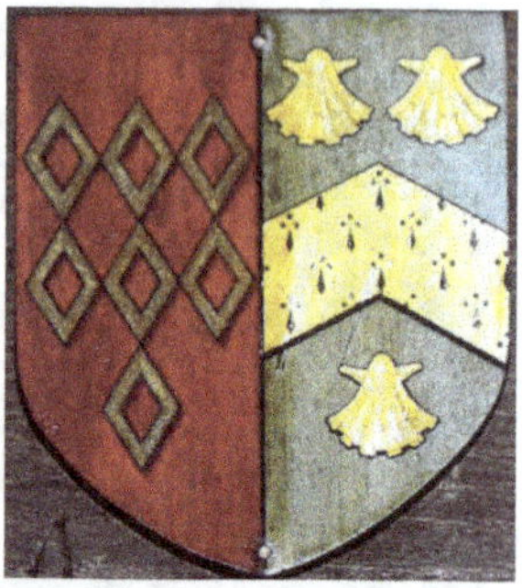   G* imp. Townshend

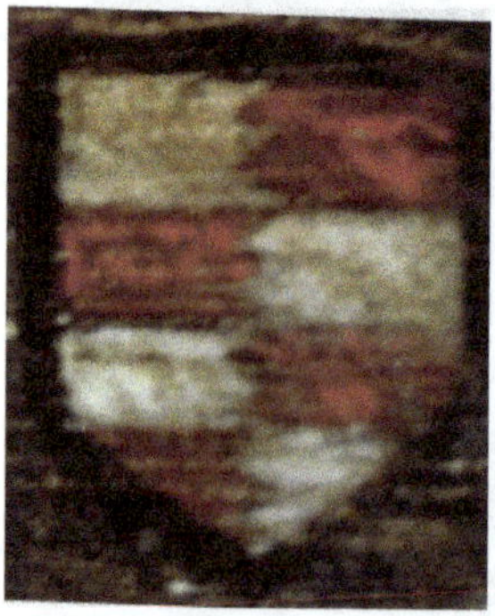

Peyto 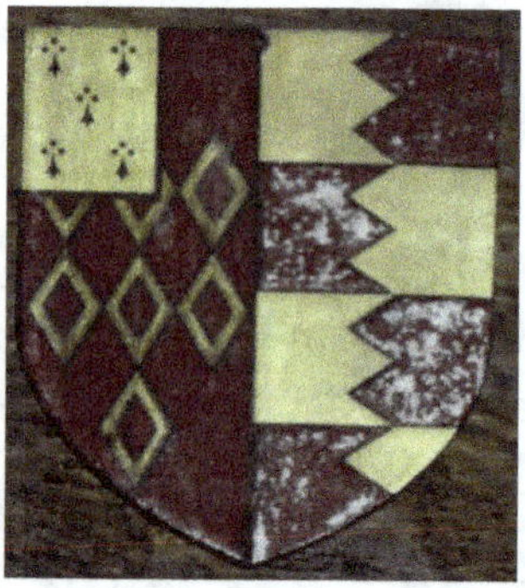   BC imp. Peyto 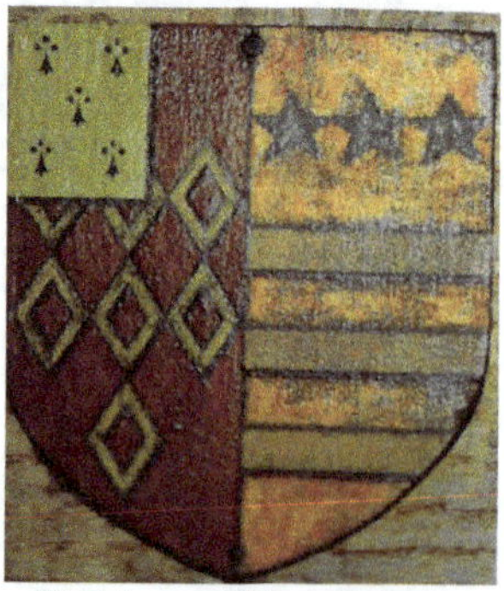   BC imp. Kempson

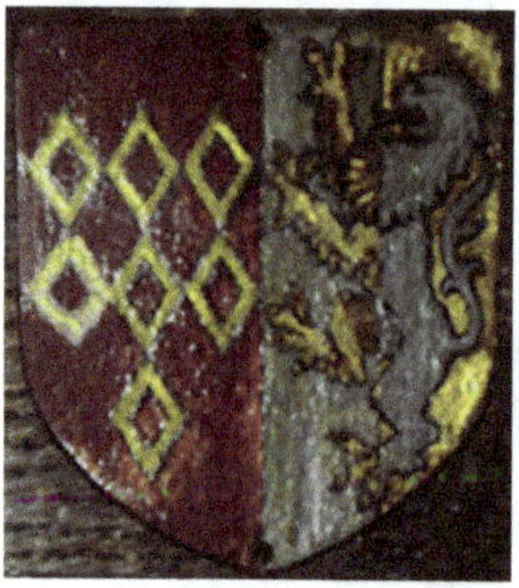

Left: BC imp. Orpen

Right: BC imp. Brome

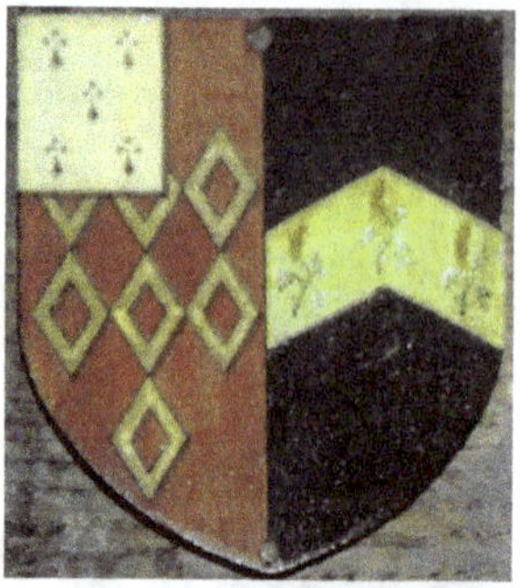

Right - Over the door leading into the Blue Bedroom is the faint outline of what appears to be the Arms of Peyto:

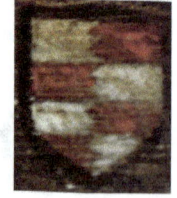

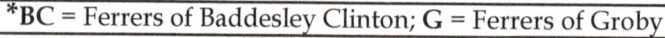

*BC = Ferrers of Baddesley Clinton; G = Ferrers of Groby

30

The Blue Bedroom:

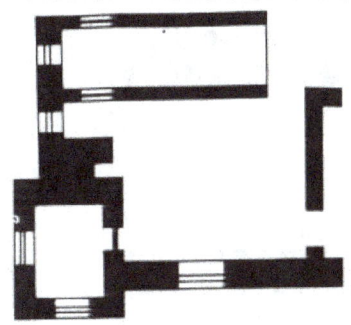

Thomas Ferrers-Walker had the Ferrers and Walker Crests engraved on a pair of silver-backed hair brushes.

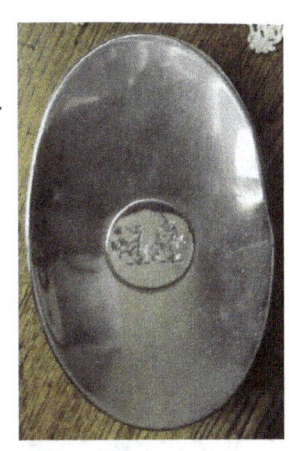

Window - left-hand pane:

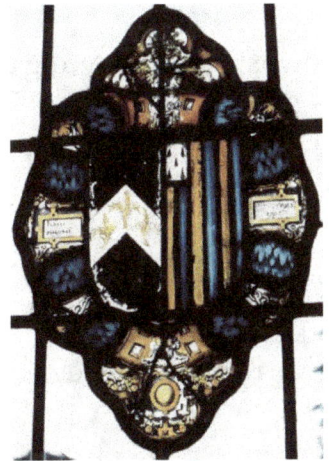

Brome imp. Shirley for John Brome (g.f. of Constance and f. of Nicholas who m. Beatrix, d. of Sir Raffe Shirley

right-hand pane:

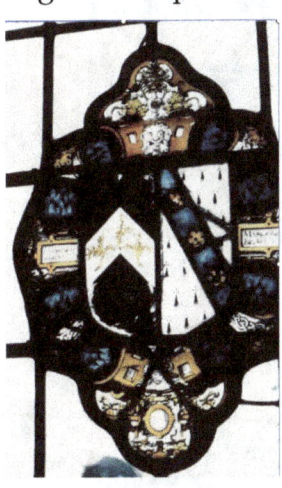

Brome imp. Beaufoy for Edward Brome and Margarie Beaufoe (sic).

Tower or Powder Room off the Blue Bedroom:

For Sir Thomas Whyte, g/f of Jane Whyte.

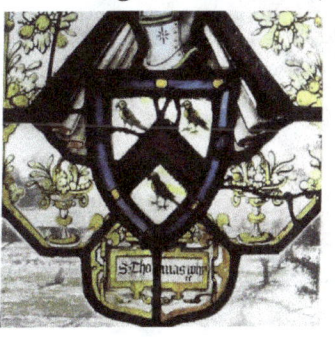

The Sacristy:
above a painting and on 2 ceiling bosses:

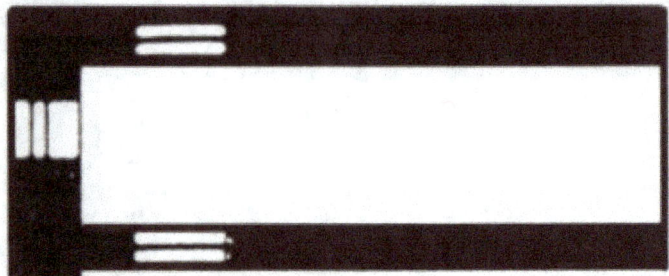

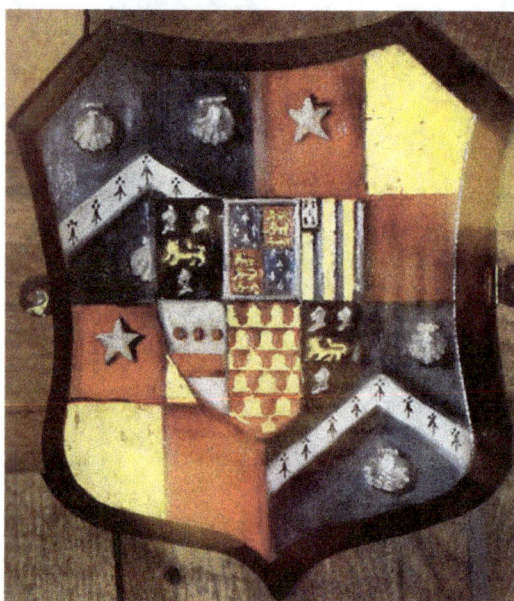

Townshend quartering de Vere
in pretence:
Qtly of 6
1.&6. Compton
2. Thomas of Woodstock
3. Shirley
4. Dering
5. Ferrers of Chartley

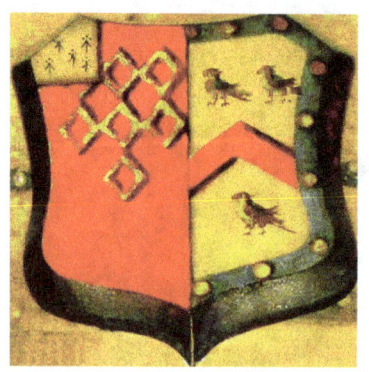

Ferrers of Baddesley Clinton
impaling Whyte.

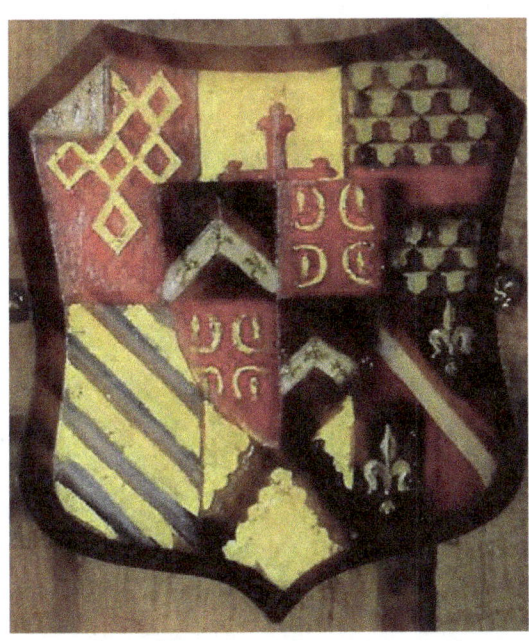

Qtly of 6
1. Ferrers of Baddesley Clinton
2. Frevill
3. Marmion
4. Mountford
5. Botetort
5. Heckstall

in pretence
Brome quartering Rhody

The Chapel:

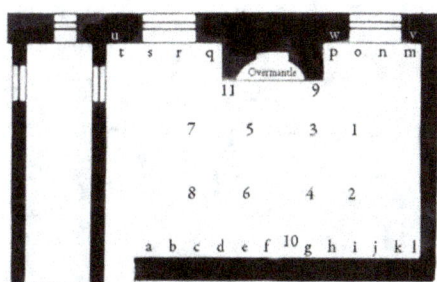

It is ablaze with shields, all painted by Rebecca Dering and showing the Arms of the Dering and Ferrers families who fought on opposite sides at the Battle of Hastings.
8 shields are placed in the cross formed by the roof beams.

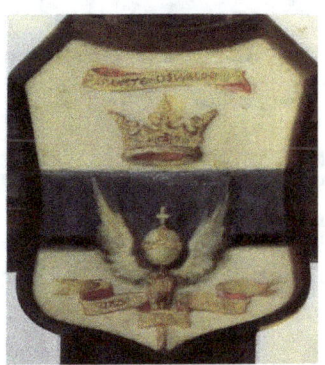

Left: Oswald, King of Deira

Right: Scotland, impaling the attributed Arms of Edward the Confessor.

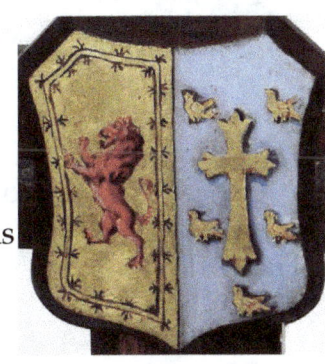

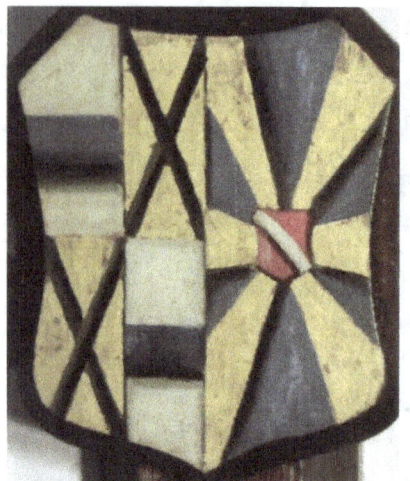

The quartered Arms of
Dering impaling
Bassingborne
with Foliot in pretence.

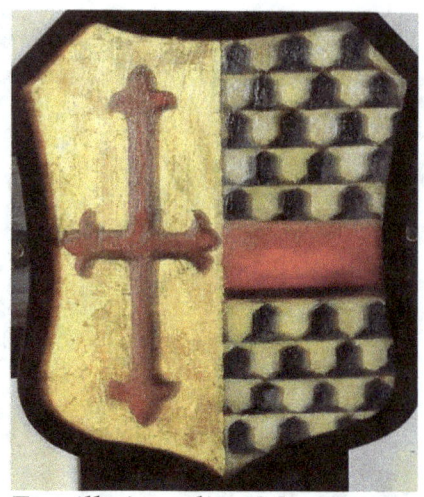

Freville impaling Marmion

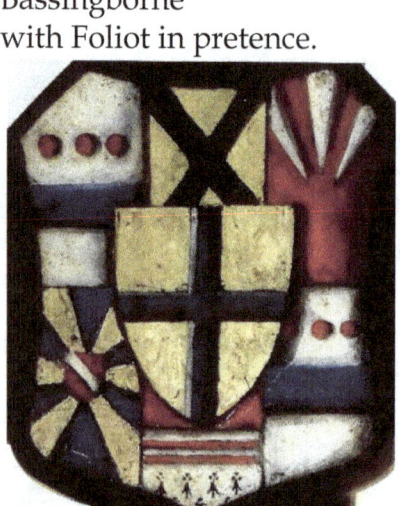

Qtly of 6
1,2 & 6. Dering
3. Hayden
4. Bassingbotne + Foliot
5. Rafe de Badlesmere (Kent)
with de Bohun in pretence.

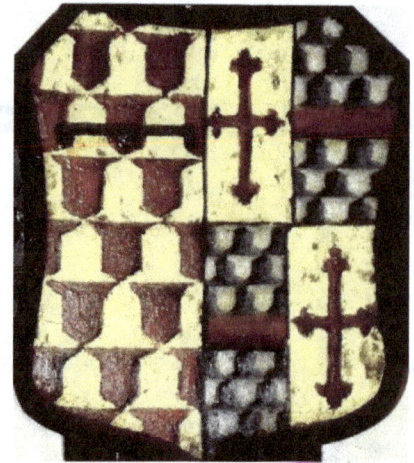

Ferrers of Chartley with a label
of 3 points impaling Frevill
quartering Marmion.
For Sir Thomas Ferrers (second
son of the 6th Lord Ferrers)
who married Elizabeth Frevill,
the heiress of Tamworth
Castle.

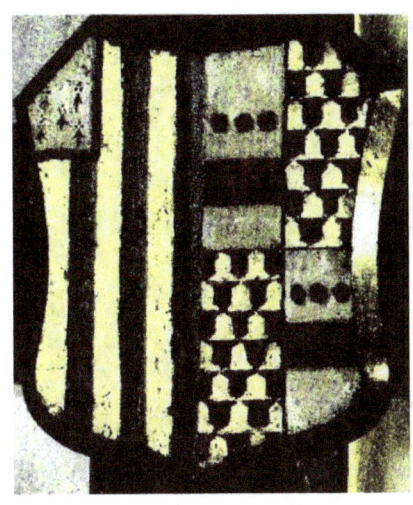

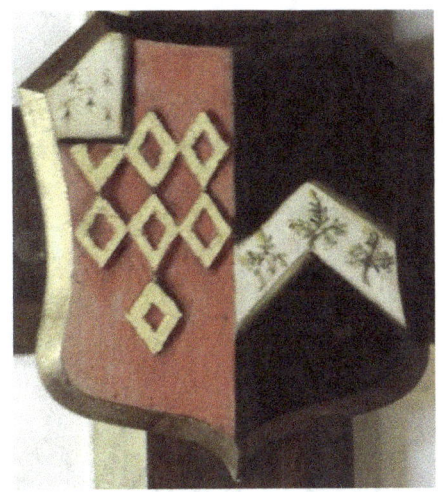

Shirley impaling
Devereux quartering Ferrers
of Chartley.

Ferrers of BC
impaling Brome.

On the **Overmantle**

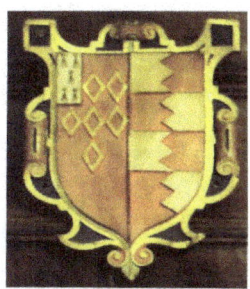

are the Arms of
Ferrers of BC
impaling Peyto.

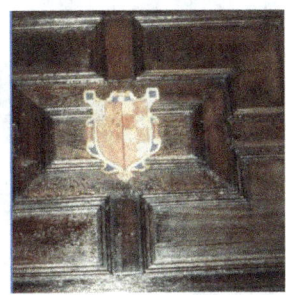

On the left cornice are the quarterly Arms of Dering
with Iremonger in pretence

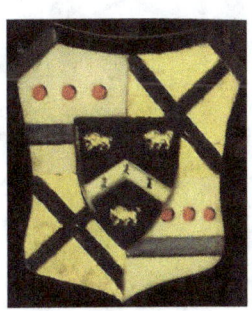

To the right
are the
attributed
Arms of
Edward the
Confessor:

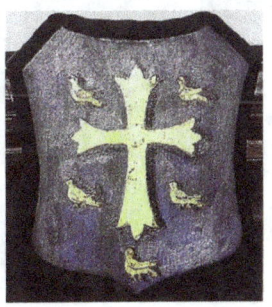

On the opposite side of the room is another shield on the cornice showing Ferrers impaling Orpen.

Quarterly of 4

1&4. Ferrers of Chartley
2. Compton of Northants.
3. Ferrers of Groby
impaling Orpen quartering Chatterton:

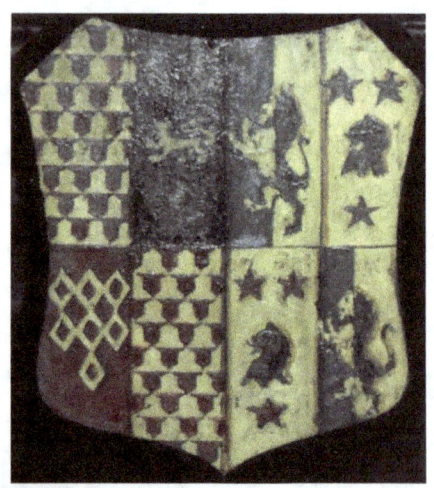

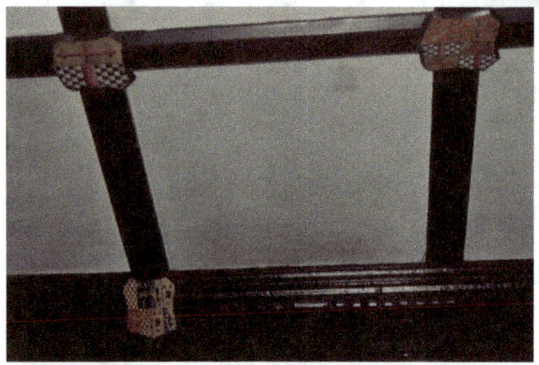

See if you can find where this photograph was taken?

We now move to the series of wooden shields.
Anticlockwise from the entrance we have:

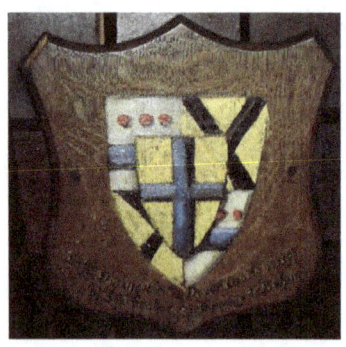

Dering with de Bohun in pretence

Ferrers, BC imp. Hampden

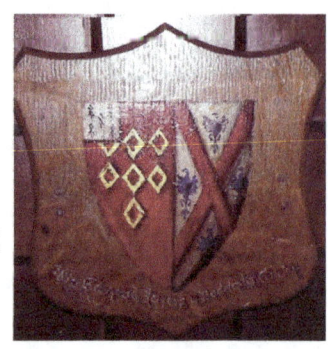

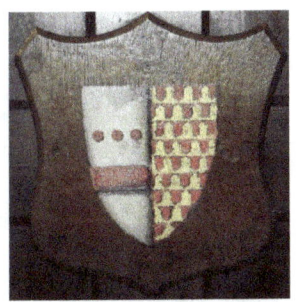

Devereux imp.
Ferrers of Chartley.

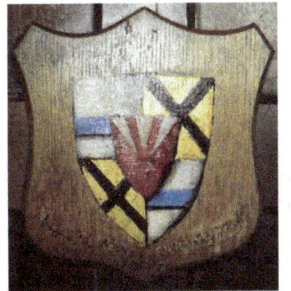

Dering with
Hayden in pretence.

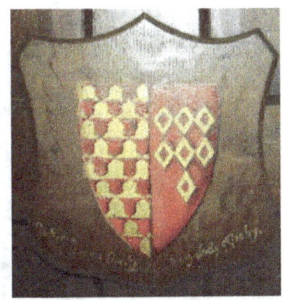

Ferrers of
Chartley imp.
Ferrers of Groby.

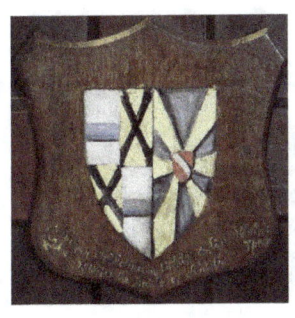

Dering imp. Bass-
ingbourne with
Foliot in pretence.

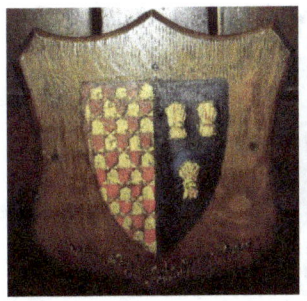

Ferrers of Chartley
imp Chester (de
Kevelick).

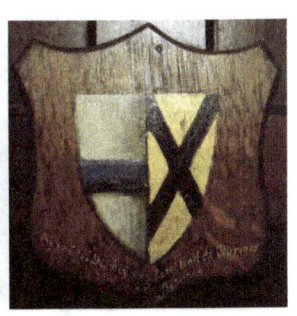

Dering imp
Molines.

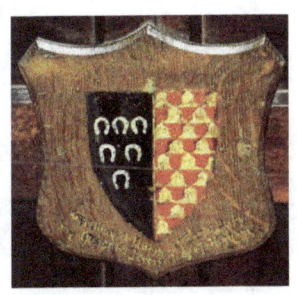

Ferrers anc. imp.
Margaret Peverel

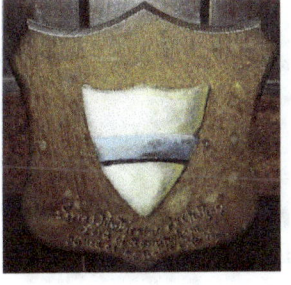

Dering (ancient).

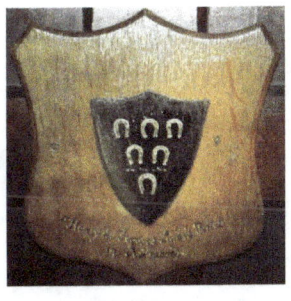

Ferrers (ancient).

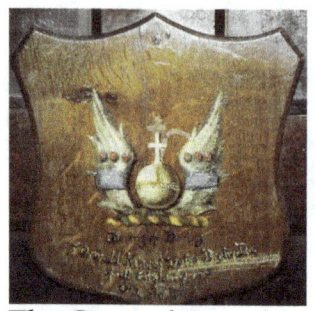

On the opposite wall to the right of the **Overmantle** the shields continue with:

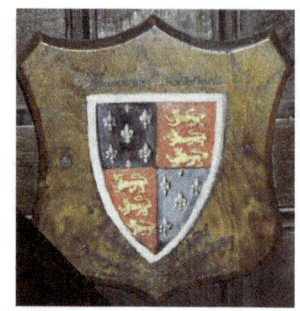

The Crest of Oswald, King of Deira - on a Torse of 10 twists (usually there are 6).

Thomas of Woodstock.

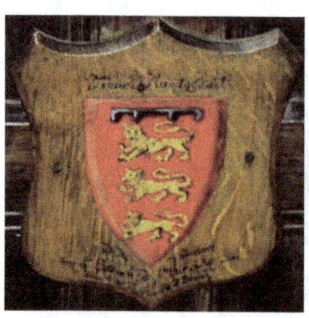

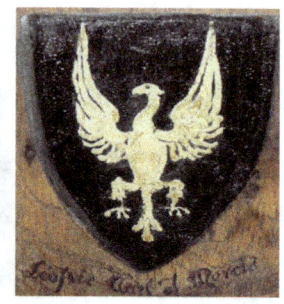

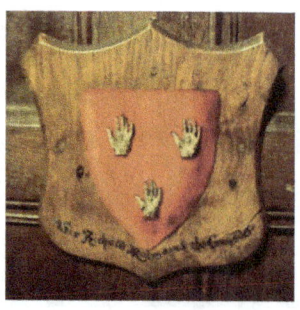

Lionel Plantagenet, 2nd surviving son of Edw.III. England - with a label of 4 points Azure.

The attributed Arms of Leofric Earl of Mercia.

Sir Richard Malmains.

and the final 4 on the other side;

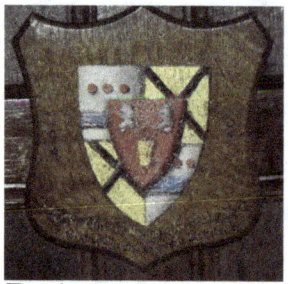

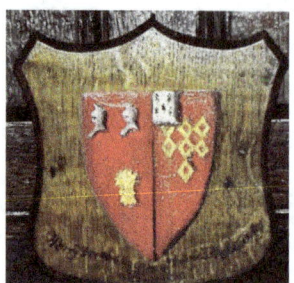

Dering with Cholmondeley in pretence.

Cholmondeley imp. Ferrers of BC.

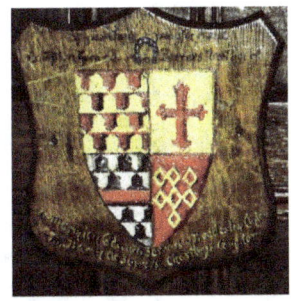

Compton Gerard Ferrers
Qtly of 4:
1. Ferrers of Chartley
2. Frevill
3. Marmion
4. Ferrers of Groby.

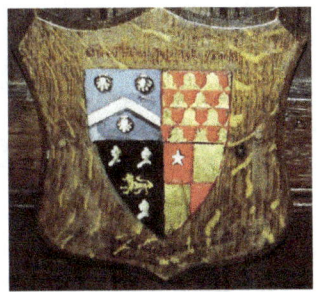

Lord Charles Vere Compton
Ferrers Townshend and
Charlotte, his wife:
Qtly of 4:
1. Townshend
2. Ferrers of Chartley
3. Compton
4. de Vere.

On the left window jamb is:

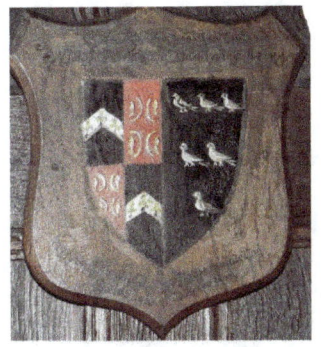

and on the right:

Left:

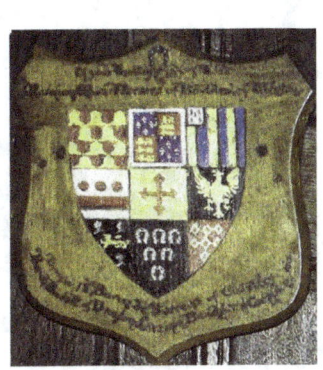

The Brome, Rhody
quartered coat imp. the
canting Arms of
Arundel
("Hirondelle" is the French
for a swallow - although
these are heraldically called
Martlets.)

Marmion Edward Ferrers of BC.
Qtly of 9:
1. Ferrers of Chartley
2. Woodstock
3. Shirley
4. Devereux
5. Frevill
6. Leofric
7. Compton
8. Ferrers anc.
9. Ferrers of Groby.

and
Right

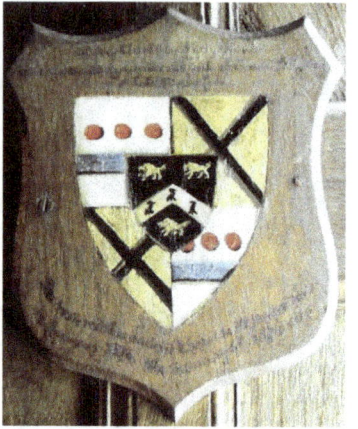

For Georgiana:
Dering
with Iremonger
in pretence.

On the **Sacristy Door** is:

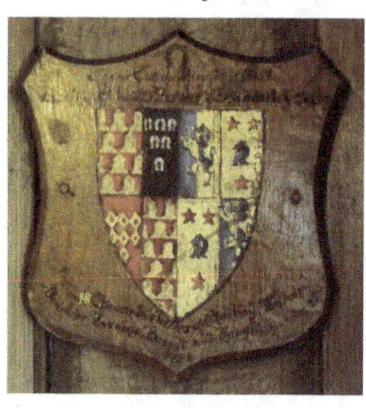

For Marmion Edward Ferrers
of BC:
Qtly of 4;
1 & 4. Ferrers of Chartley
2. Ferrers anc.
3. Ferrers of Groby
impaling
Orpen quartering Chatterton
(for his wife Rebecca Dulcibella
Orpen).

Originally in the Chapel these 2 shields of lady's Arms (on a
lozenge) have now been placed over the top of the stairs to the
Upper Landing:

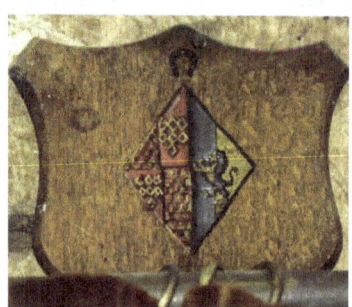

Qtly of 4:
1&4. Ferrers of
Chartley
2&3. Ferrers of
Groby
imp. Orpen.

Ferrers of BC
imp. Townshend.

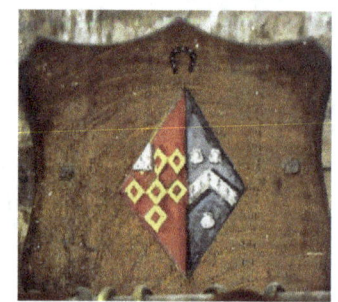

We now climb the stairs to the **Upper Corridor**:

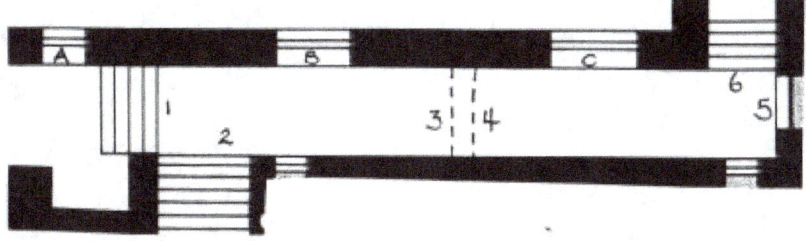

Over the stairs is the unicorn Crest of Ferrers:

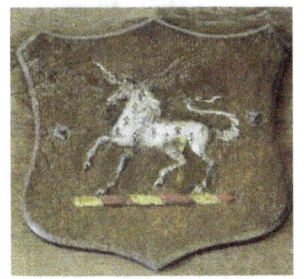

The Dering Crest is over the stairs:

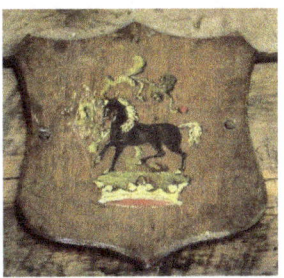

On either side of the central beam are:

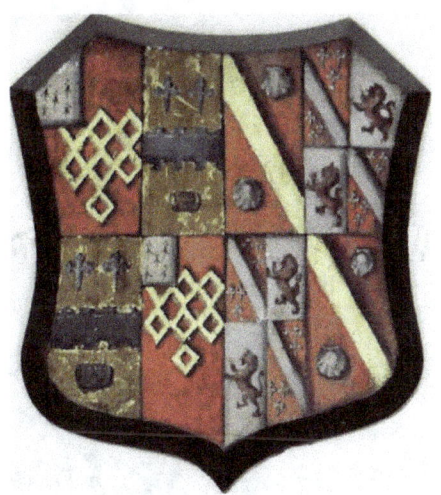

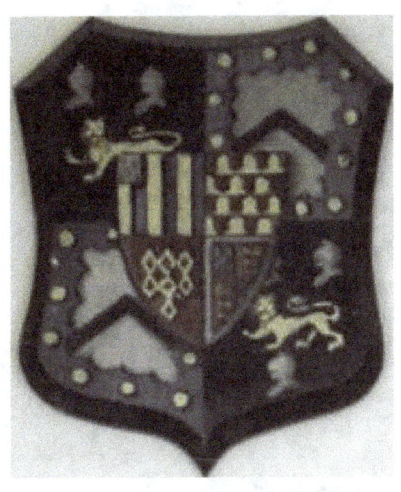

Ferrers of BC qrtg Croxon imp. Petre qrtg Howard (which in turn is Howard qtrg Ormsby).

Compton qtrg Vannell with Qtly Shirley, Ferrers of Chartley, Ferrers of Groby and Woodstock in pretence.

Back down at the end of the Corridor are:

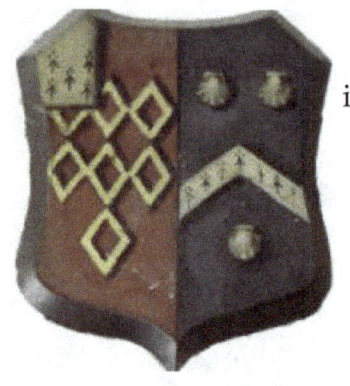

Ferrers of BC
imp Townshend.

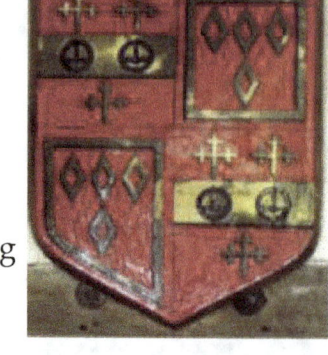

Ferrers qtrg
Walker.

There are 3 windows, each with two coats. Up the steps on the
left is **Window A**:

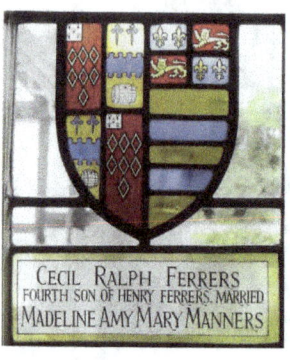

CECIL RALPH FERRERS
FOURTH SON OF HENRY FERRERS. MARRIED
MADELINE AMY MARY MANNERS

Ferrers of BC qtrg
Croxon
imp Manners

Ferrers of BC
qtrg Croxon.

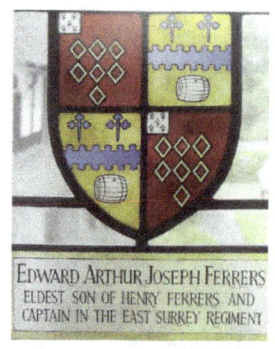

EDWARD ARTHUR JOSEPH FERRERS
ELDEST SON OF HENRY FERRERS AND
CAPTAIN IN THE EAST SURREY REGIMENT

Window B:

> * When the charges on a shield are a
> reference/rebus of the armiger.
> Here we have Cross(es) on a Tun.

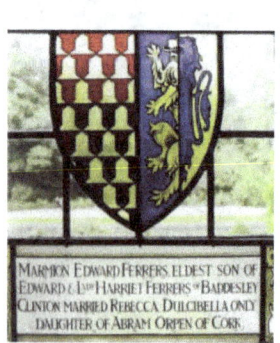

MARMION EDWARD FERRERS ELDEST SON OF
EDWARD & LADY HARRIET FERRERS OF BADDESLEY
CLINTON MARRIED REBECCA DULCIBELLA ONLY
DAUGHTER OF ABRAM ORPEN OF CORK

Ferrers of
Chartley imp
Orpen.

The canting
Arms* of
Croxon imp
Ferrers of BC.

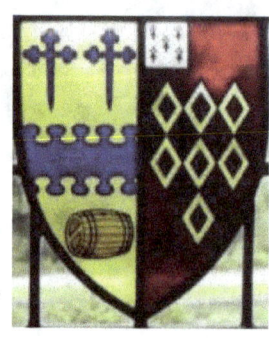

Window C:

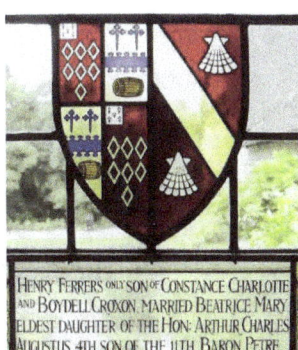

HENRY FERRERS ONLY SON OF CONSTANCE CHARLOTTE AND BOYDELL CROXON, MARRIED BEATRICE MARY ELDEST DAUGHTER OF THE HON: ARTHUR CHARLES AUGUSTUS 4TH SON OF THE 11TH BARON PETRE.

Ferrers of BC qrtg Croxon imp Petre

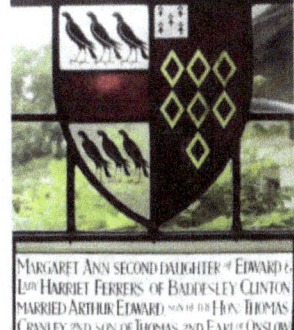

MARGARET ANN SECOND DAUGHTER of EDWARD & L^DY HARRIET FERRERS OF BADDESLEY CLINTON MARRIED ARTHUR EDWARD SON OF THE HON: THOMAS CRANLEY, 2ND SON OF THOMAS 2ND EARL OF ONSLOW

Cranley imp. Ferrers of BC

Study - now used as an Office and may not be open to the public. There are 2 windows each with 2 lights:

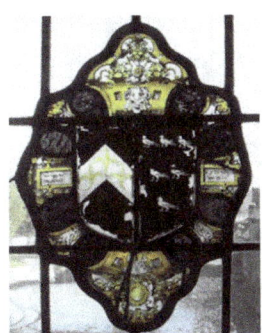

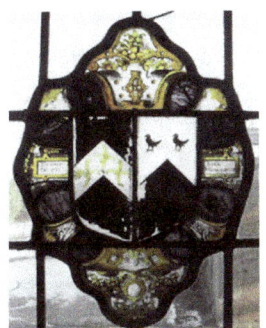

L. Brome imp. Arundel.

R. Brome imp. Middlemore.

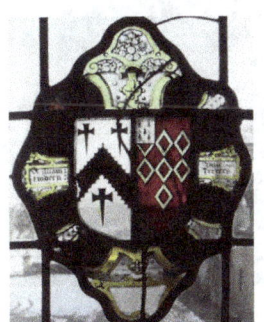

L: Findern imp. Ferrers of BC.

R: Knightly imp. Ferrers of BC.

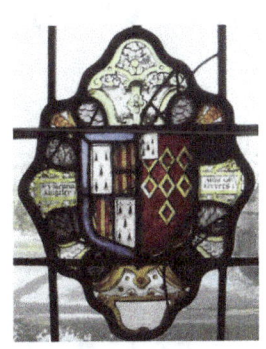

The Library:

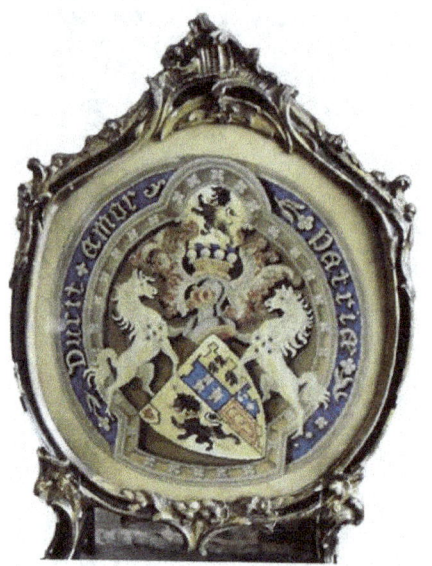

On the firescreen is probably:
Meredith of Radnor imp.
Qtly: 1. The Duke of Gordon
2. Badenoch
3. Seton
4. Frazer.

Walker qrtg Ferrers
Commissioned by
Thomas Ferrers-Walker
but the artist is unknown
to me and I forgot to ask.

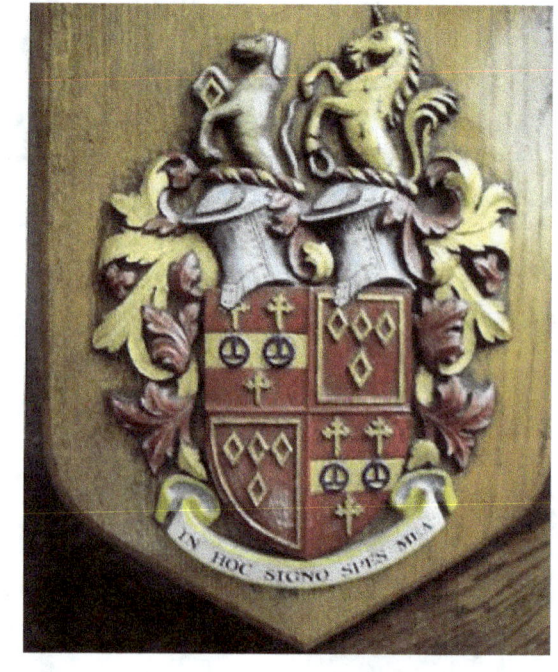

"Odds and Sods!" - found in and around the house:

Georgian silver.

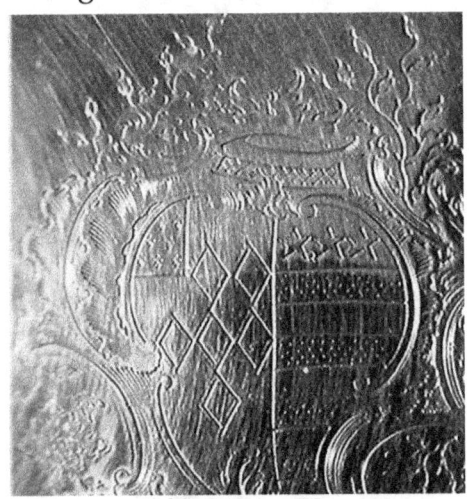

Ferrers of BC imp. Kempson.

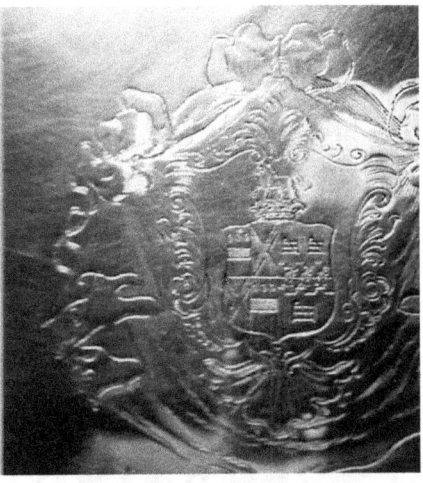

Dering imp. Y(e)ates.

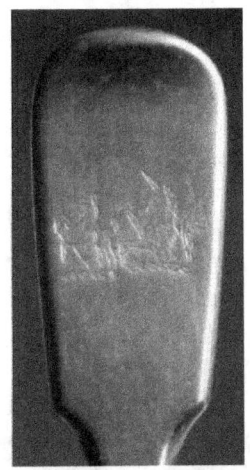

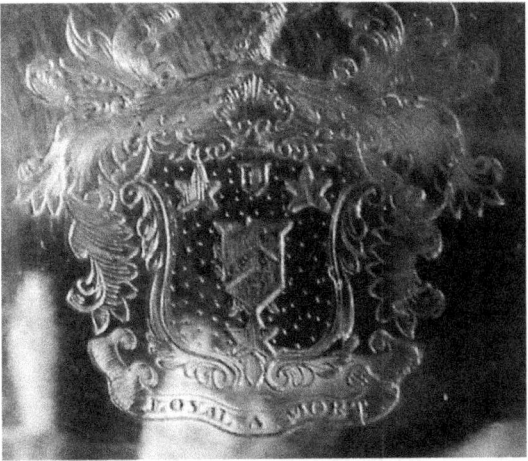

Thomas Ferrers-Walker had a set of spoons engraved with the Ferrers-Walker Crests.
They are probably still in the **Dining Room.**

As is the silver tureen with Chatterton (with the Red hand of Ulster)
and Iremonger in pretence.

On the lock on the **Chapel Door** are 2 unicorns "affronty" (facing one another). The Ferrers' Crest.

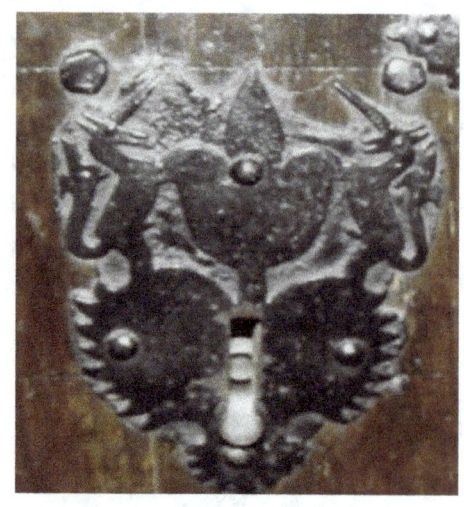

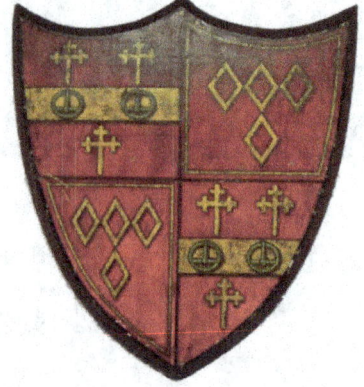

Another version of the Ferrers-Walker Arms.

As is the Cupboard on which Thomas Ferrers-Walker had had carved the new quartering of Ferrers to his Arms (Granted by the College of Arms in 1941) after his name change.

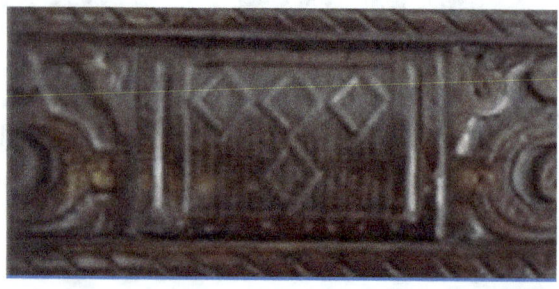

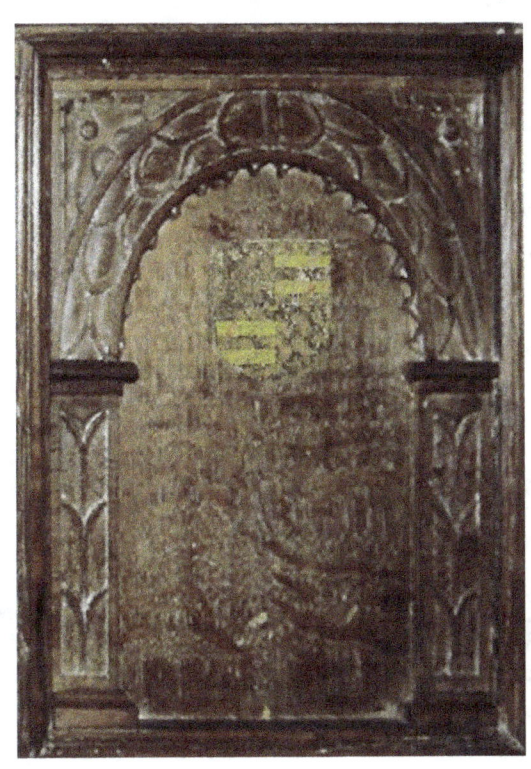

Painted directly onto the panelling in a bedtoom are some unknown quartered Arms.

A stained glass window - but its location was unknown to me.

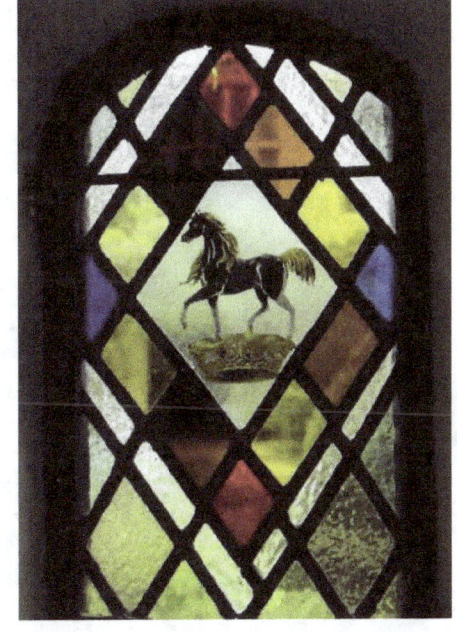

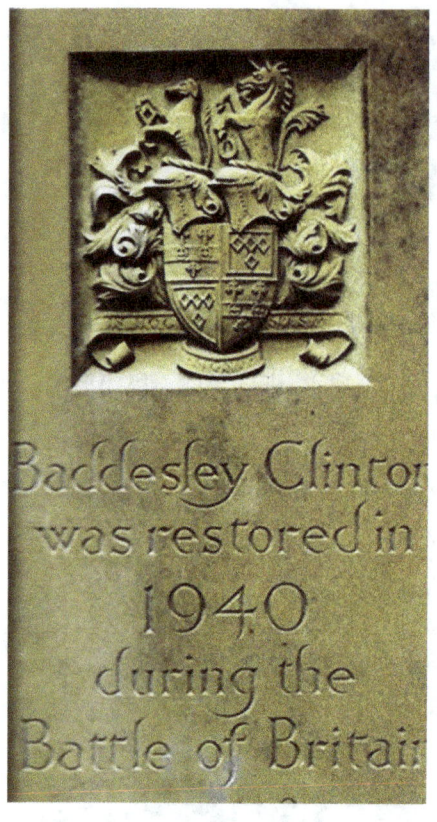

In thr Sable block:
Ferrers-Walker.

Rebecca Dering overpainted many of her family's portraits with their coats of Arms. See how many you can find?.

Many more were taken down from the Chapel during the time of its restoration but were not put back. They are probably in storage.

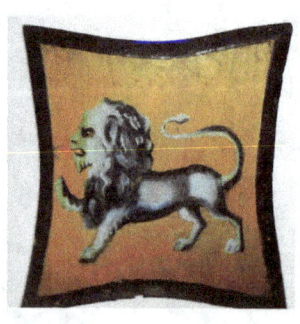 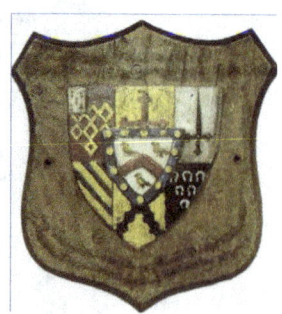 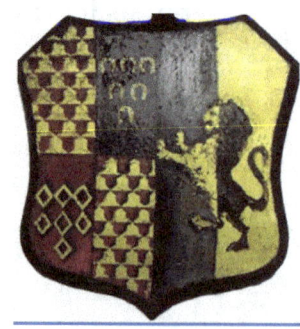

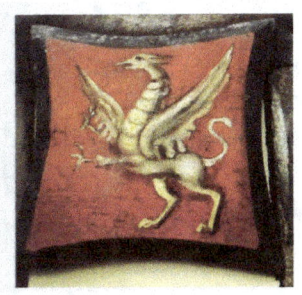 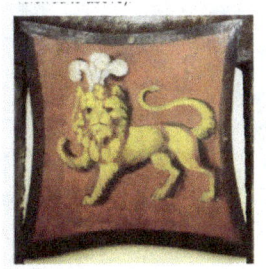 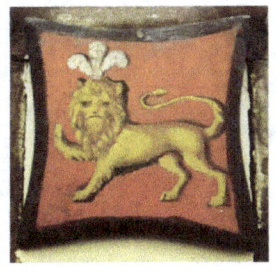

More views -
from the Chapel:

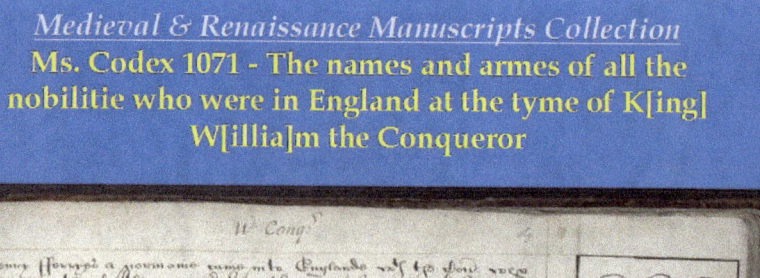

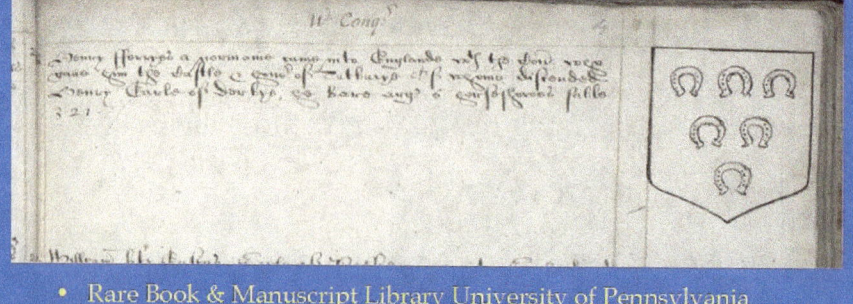

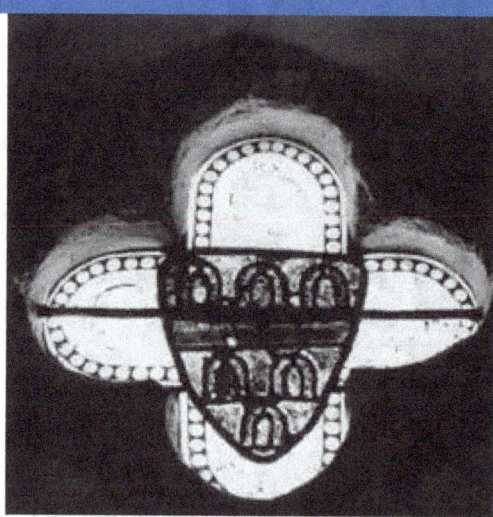

The origin of the Ferrers ancient Arms.

Above, in a rare MS

and

High up in a church window in Ferrers' country in Normandy, France.

When it came to Baddesley Clinton they reversed the tinctures.

That concludes our visit to the Manor House. We now go back down the lane and turn left for the short walk to **St Michael's Church** on our right.

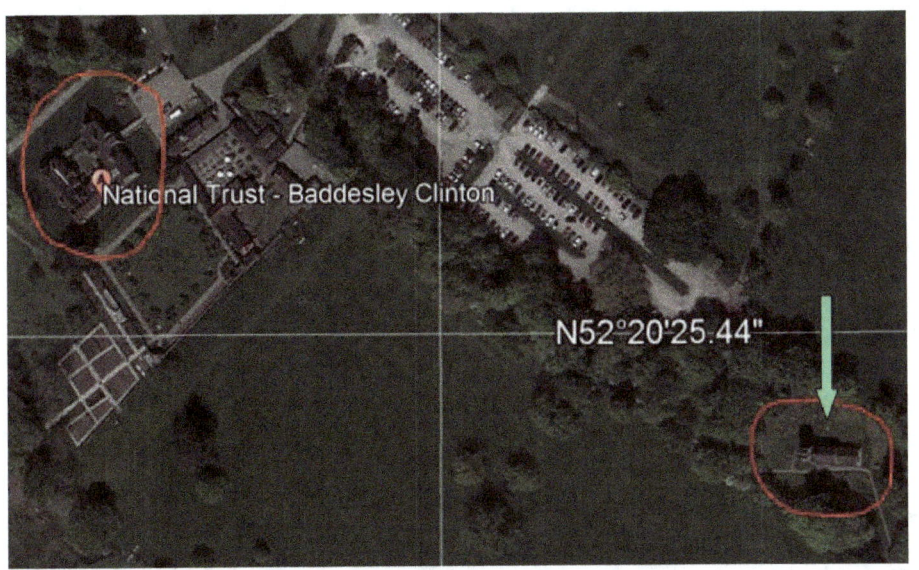

National Trust - Baddesley Clinton

N52°20'25.44"

St Michael's Church:

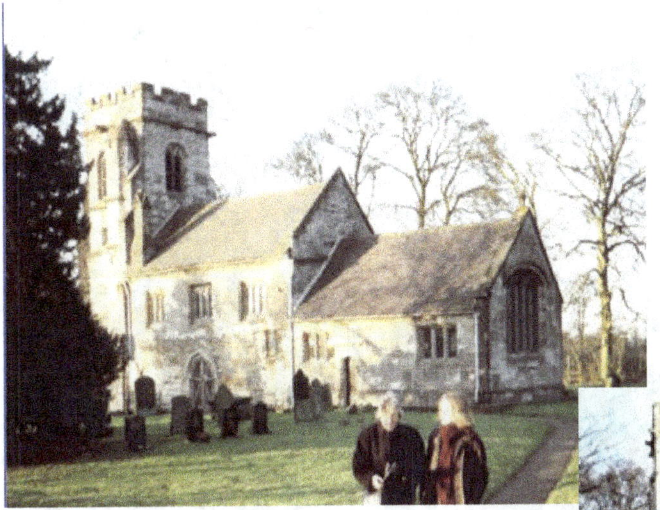

The Tower was built by Nicholas Brome.

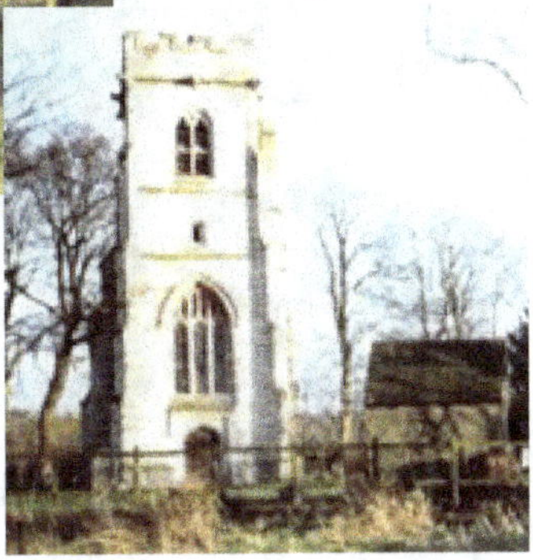

There is a floor slab which effectively states that, "I walked all over you in life so now you can walk all over me in death."

In the Tower there is a shield for Thomas "Ferrers":

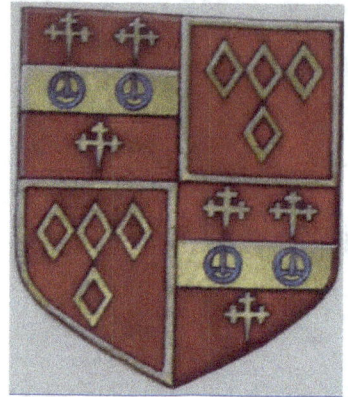

Qtly 1&4. Walker,
2&3. Ferrers.

Alongside, on the beam, are carved
the crosses crosslet fitchée & mascles
of Ferrers-Walker:

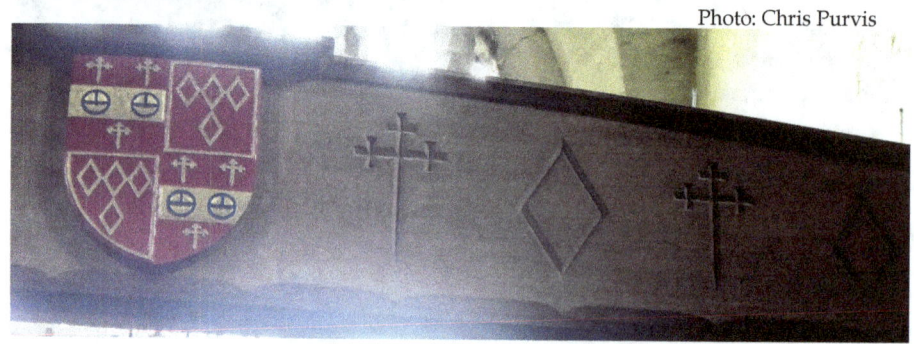

The stunning East Window

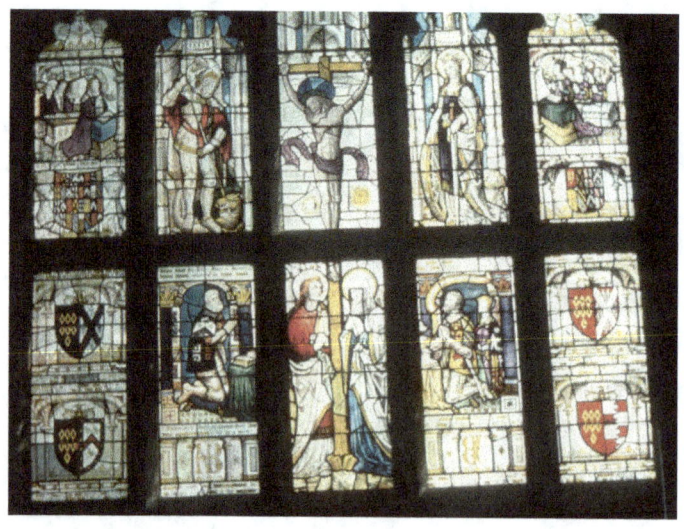

From l-r (top)

Sir Edward Ferrers of Groby
imp. Constance Brome

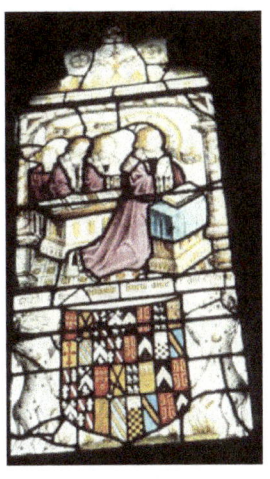

Qtly quartered   imp.   Qtly quartered

1&4. g/qtrs: 1&4. g/qtrs:
1. Ferrers of Groby   1&4. Brome
2. Botetort   2&3. Rhody
3. Frevill
4. Mountford   2&3. g/qtrs:
                        1. Arundel
2&3. g/qtrs: 2. Courtenay
1&4. Heckstall   3. Coleshill
2&3. Hewett   4. Carminow

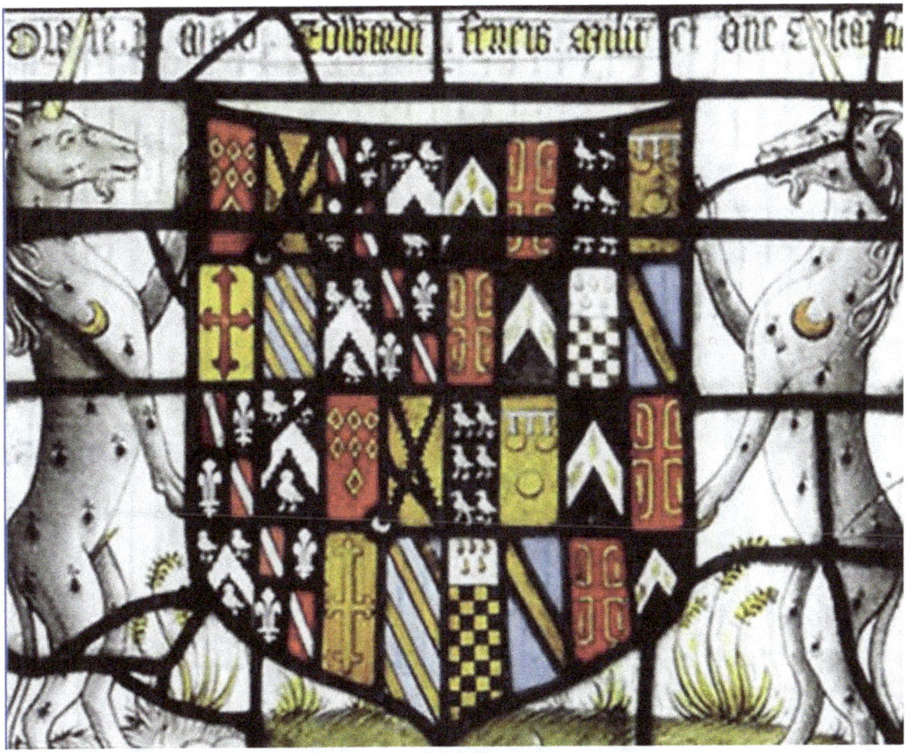

Upper right-hand:

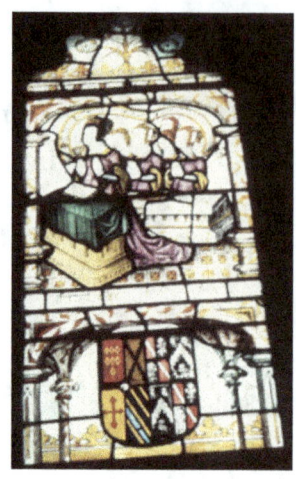

Sir Edward Ferrers of Groby:

Constance Brome:

Qtly of 4:
1. Ferrers of Groby
2. Botetort
3. Frevill
4. Mountford
(a crescent for difference.
The cadency mark of a second son.).

Below her are the Arms of Margaret Heckstall, her mother-in-law:

Heckstall qtrg Hewitt.

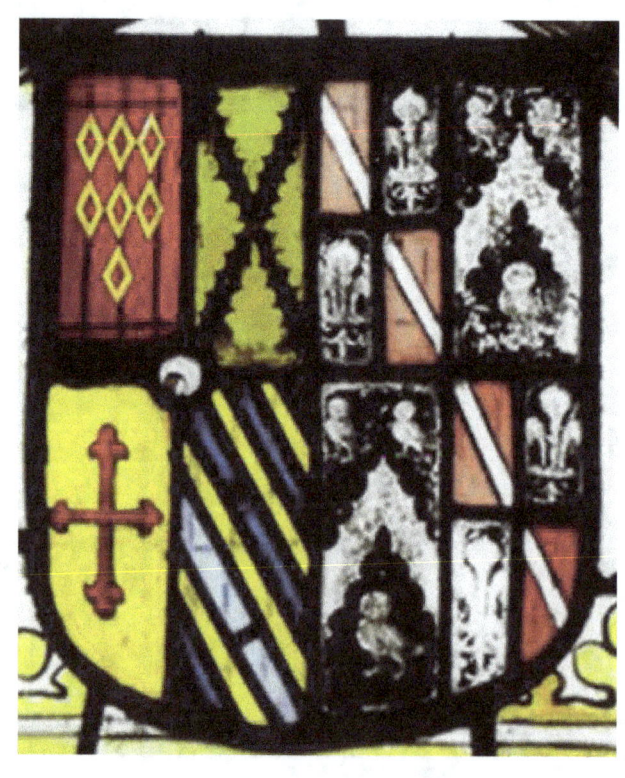

from l-r (bottom)

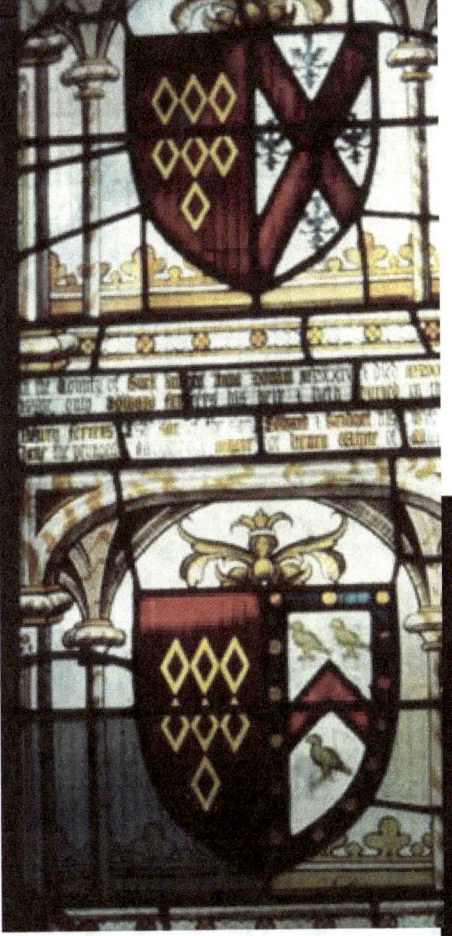

Henry Ferrers (Groby)
imp. Katherine Hampden

Henry Ferrers (Groby)
imp. Jane Whyte

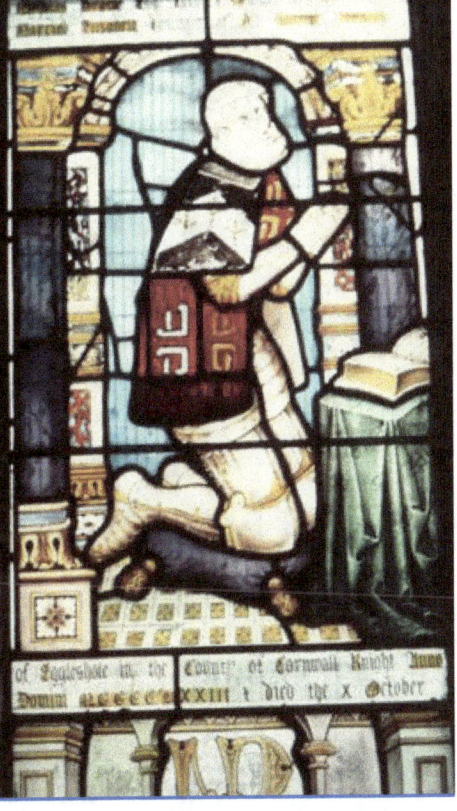

Nicholas Brome wearing a
tabard of Brome quartering
Rody

"Gules a cross moline voided
betw. four fishes houriant Or"

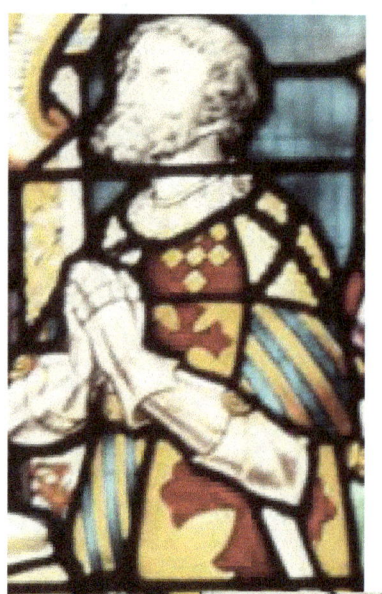

Sir Edward Ferrers of
Groby
with his wife
Constance Brome

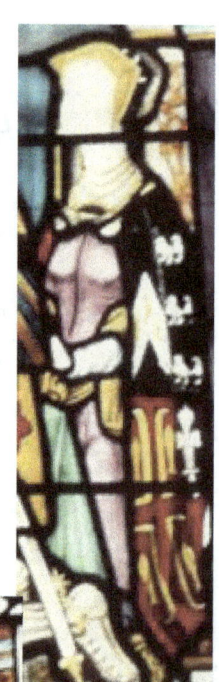

Each wearing tabards
of the impaled Arms
shown above.

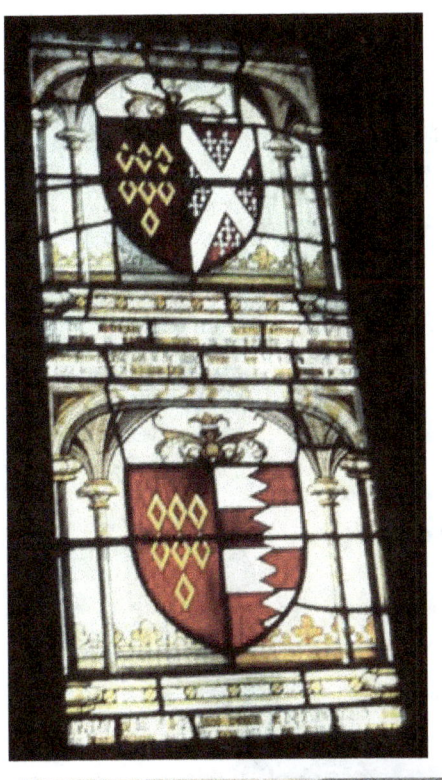

Edward Ferrers (Groby)
imp.
 Bridget Windsor

Edward Ferrers (Groby)
imp.
  Anne Peyto

Strictly non heraldic but
there for the record - on a
floor plate::

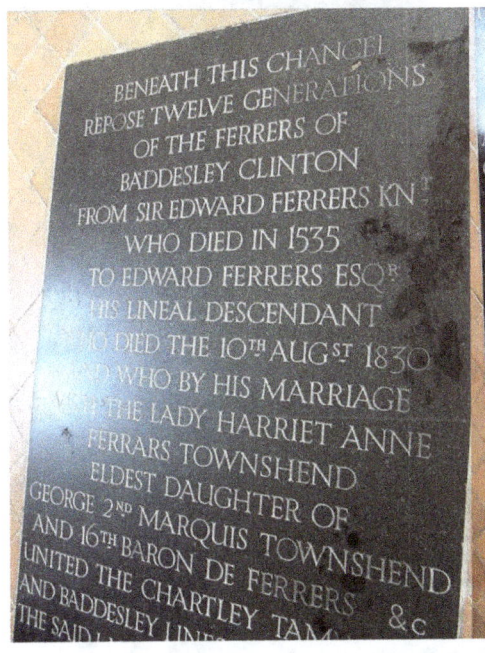

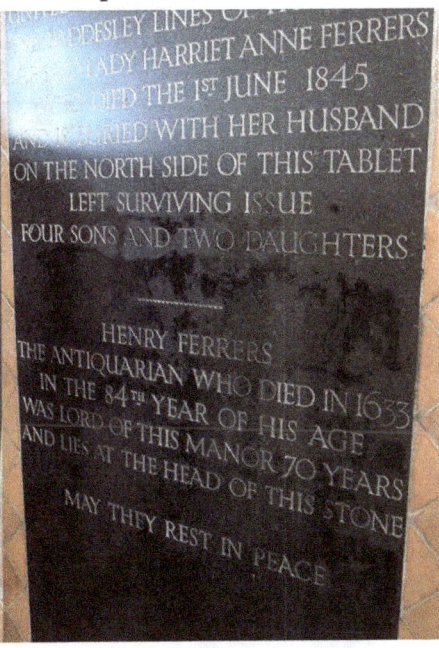

BENEATH THIS CHANCEL
REPOSE TWELVE GENERATIONS
OF THE FERRERS OF
BADDESLEY CLINTON
FROM SIR EDWARD FERRERS KNᵀ
WHO DIED IN 1535
TO EDWARD FERRERS ESQᴿ
HIS LINEAL DESCENDANT
WHO DIED THE 10ᵀᴴ AUGˢᵀ 1830
AND WHO BY HIS MARRIAGE
WITH THE LADY HARRIET ANNE
FERRARS TOWNSHEND
ELDEST DAUGHTER OF
GEORGE 2ᴺᴰ MARQUIS TOWNSHEND
AND 16ᵀᴴ BARON DE FERRERS
UNITED THE CHARTLEY TAM &ᶜ
AND BADDESLEY LINES
THE SAID L...

BADDESLEY LINES OF
LADY HARRIET ANNE FERRERS
DIED THE 1ˢᵀ JUNE 1845
AND IS BURIED WITH HER HUSBAND
ON THE NORTH SIDE OF THIS TABLET
LEFT SURVIVING ISSUE
FOUR SONS AND TWO DAUGHTERS

HENRY FERRERS
THE ANTIQUARIAN WHO DIED IN 1633
IN THE 84ᵀᴴ YEAR OF HIS AGE
WAS LORD OF THIS MANOR 70 YEARS
AND LIES AT THE HEAD OF THIS STONE
MAY THEY REST IN PEACE

There are 2 Funeral Hatchments

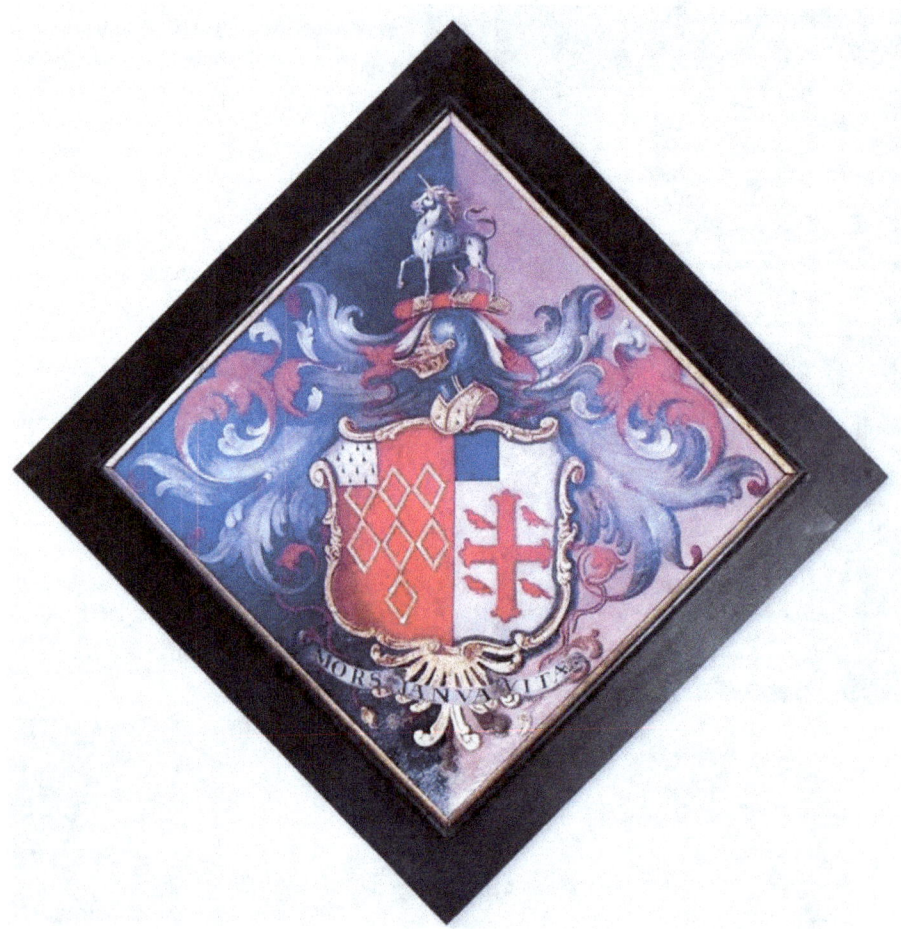

Dexter background black
Gules seven mascles conjoined three, three and one or, a canton
ermine (Ferrers), impaling, Argent a cross flory between four
martlets gules a canton azure (Bird)
Crest: A unicorn passant ermine, crined, armed and unguled or
Mantling: Gules and argent
Motto: Mors janua vitae
Skull and cross-bones in base.
For Edward Ferrers who m. Hester, dau. of Christopher Bird of
London and d. 1794.

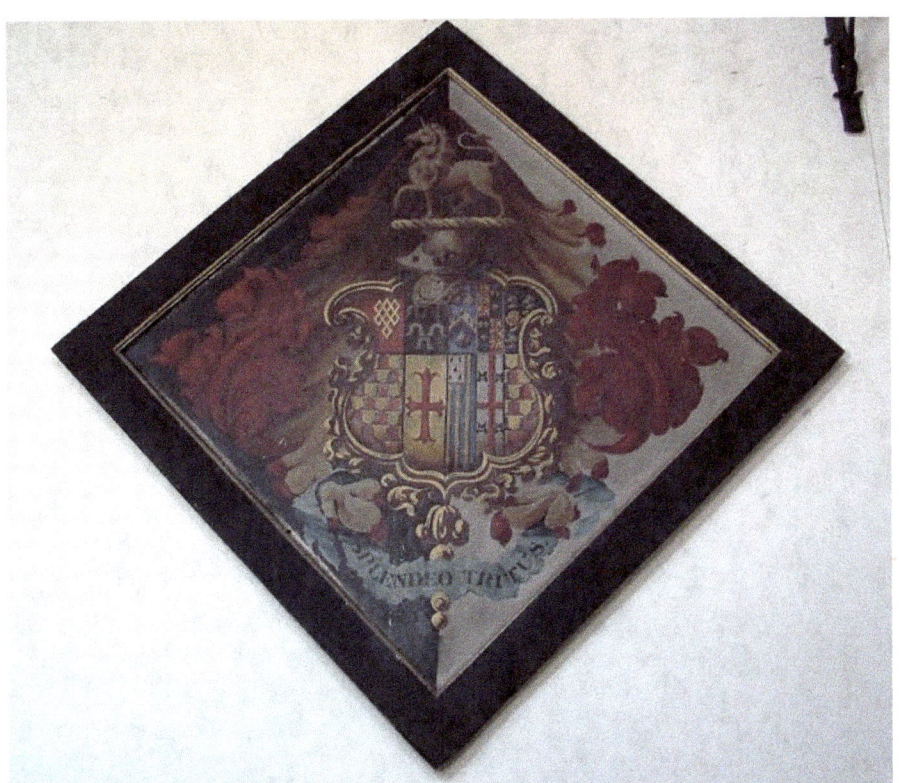

Dexter background black
Quarterly, 1st, Gules seven mascles conjoined three, three and one
or (Ferrers), 2nd, Sable six horseshoes argent (Ferrers), 3rd, Vairy or
and gules (Ferrers), 4th, Or a cross patonce gules (Freville), impaling,
Quarterly, 1st Azure a chevron ermine between three escallops argent
(Townshend), 2nd, Or three lions passant guardant gules (England,
incorrectly painted) quartering France within a bordure argent ( ),
3rd, Sable a lion passant or between three esquires' helmets argent
(Compton), 4th, Paly of six or and azure a canton ermine (Shirley),
5th, Argent a cross engrailed gules between four water bougets sable
(Bourchier), 6th, Vairy or and gules (Ferrers)
Crest: A unicorn passant proper   Mantling: Gules and argent
Motto: Splendeo tritus
For Edward Ferrers, who married 11 Mar 1813 Harriet Anne
Ferrers Townshend, 2nd daughter and co-heir of George, 2nd
Marquess Townshend, and died 10 Aug 1830;

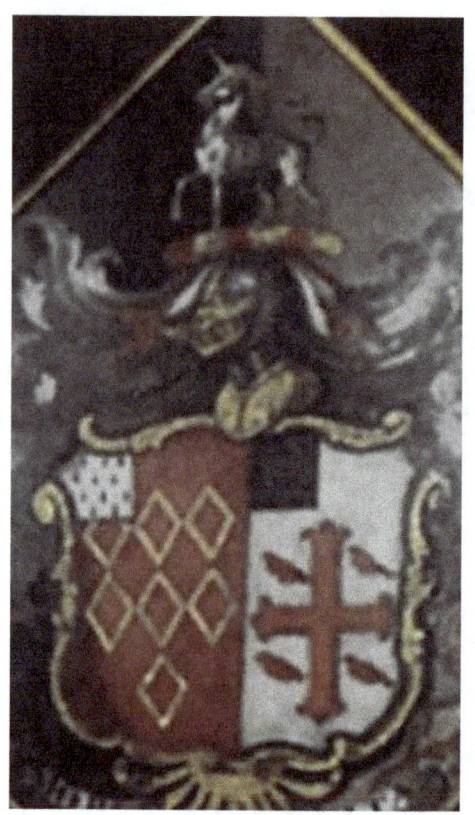 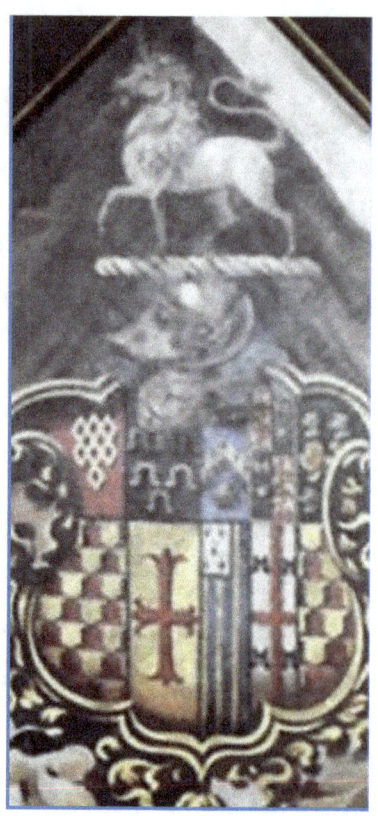

Details of the Arms shown above. Both photographs are from the
Heraldry Society's Archive Collection and the details are from
Vol. 1 of the excellent 10 volume series, *"Hatchments In Britain"*
by Peter Summers.

We now move to the magnificant, if rather water-damaged, tomb
of Sir Edward Ferrers (died 1535).

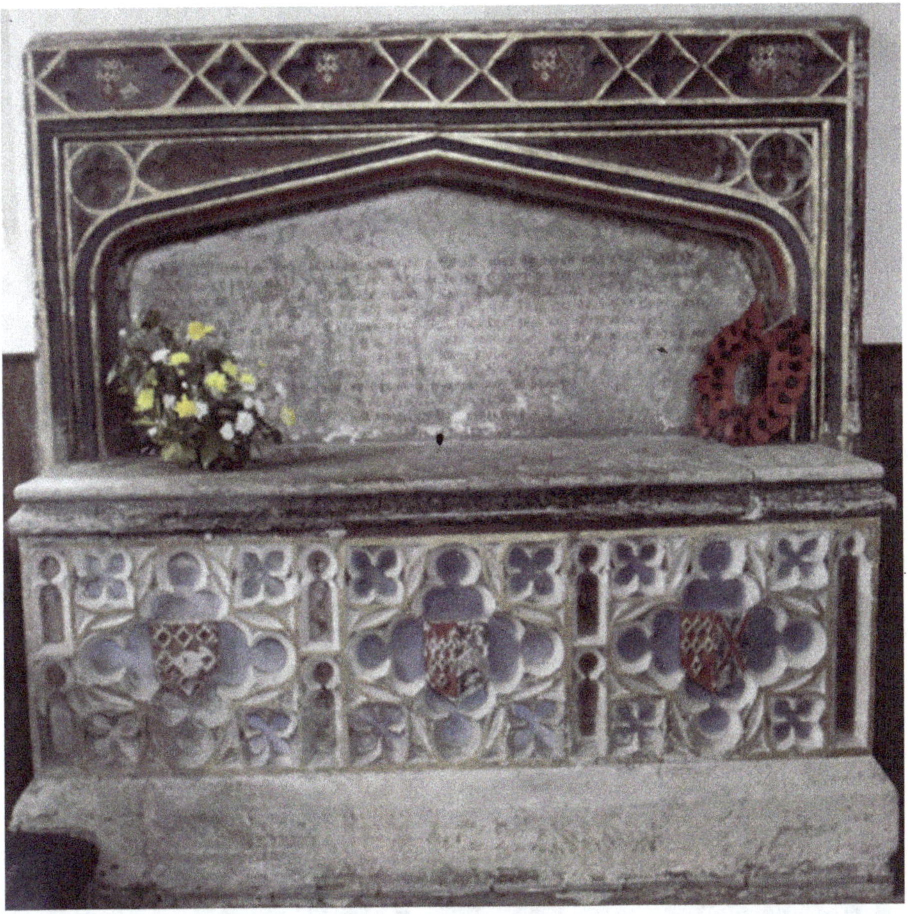

The three shields along the bottom are for our old « friends »
Ferrers of Groby, Hampden & Brome

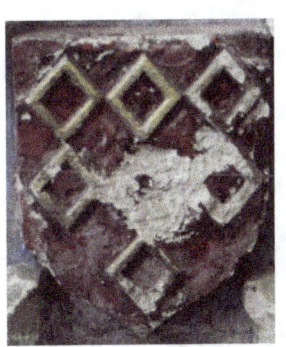
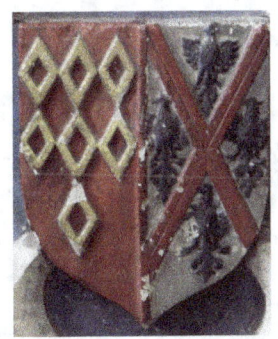
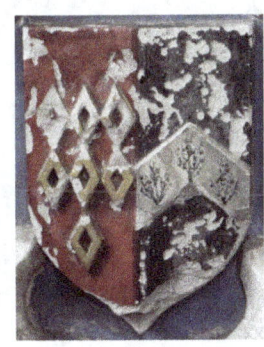

The four shields across the top are for Ferrers of Baddesley Clinton impaling:

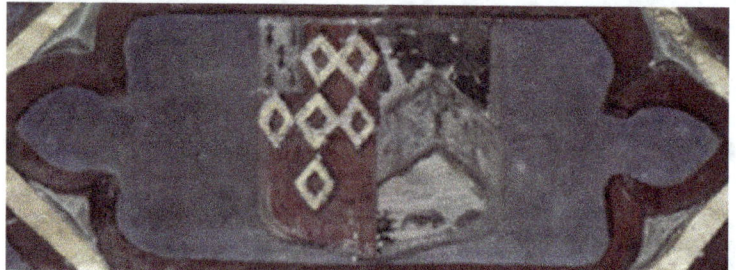

Brome

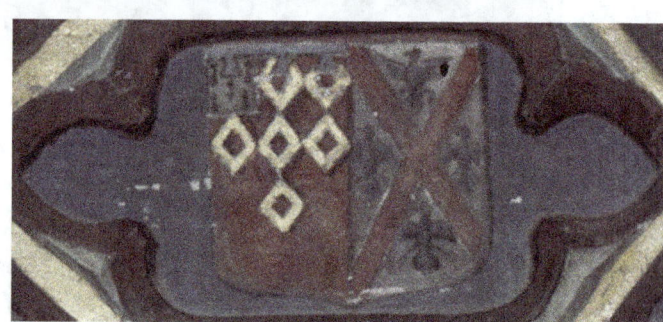

Hampden

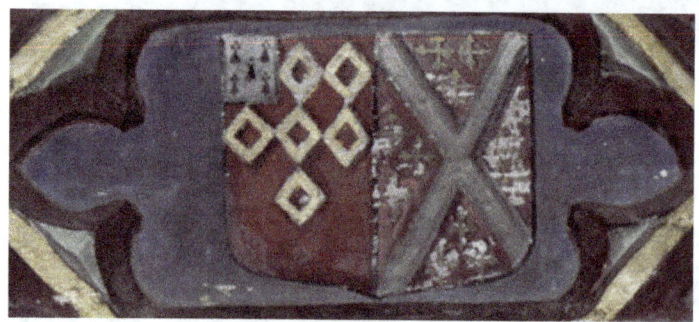

Whyte

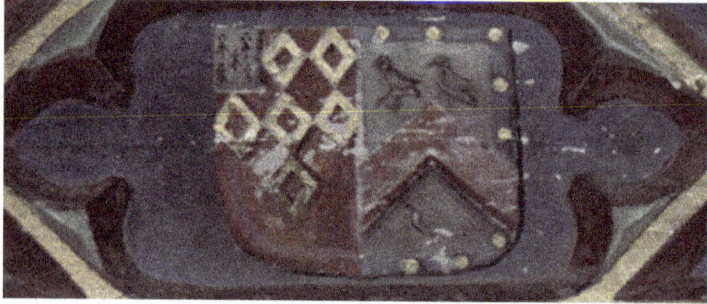

Windsor

The Wall Plaque for Edward Ferrers

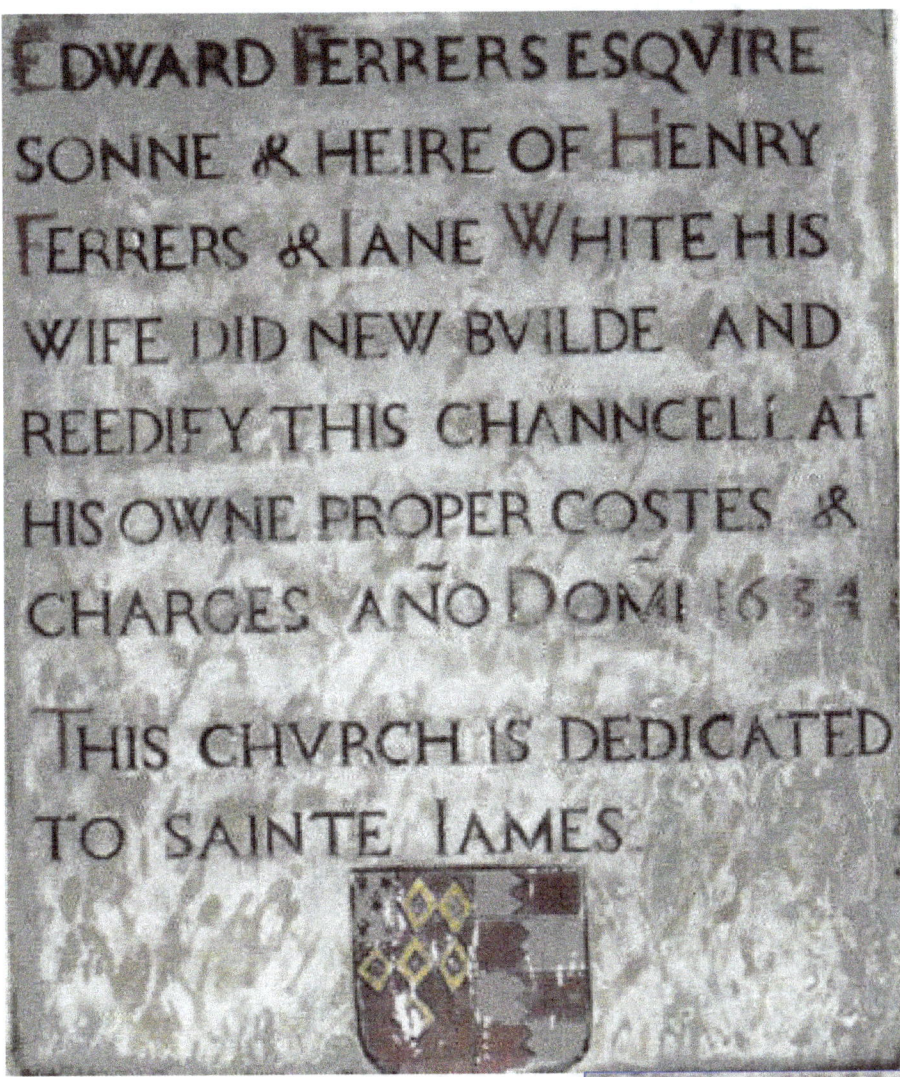

EDWARD FERRERS ESQVIRE
SONNE & HEIRE OF HENRY
FERRERS & IANE WHITE HIS
WIFE DID NEW BVILDE AND
REEDIFY THIS CHANNCELL AT
HIS OWNE PROPER COSTES &
CHARGES AÑO DOMI 1634

THIS CHVRCH IS DEDICATED
TO SAINTE IAMES

Although the plaque mentions Jane Whyte the Arms shown are for Ferrers of BC imp. Peyto:

Plaque for Thomas & Undine Ferrers

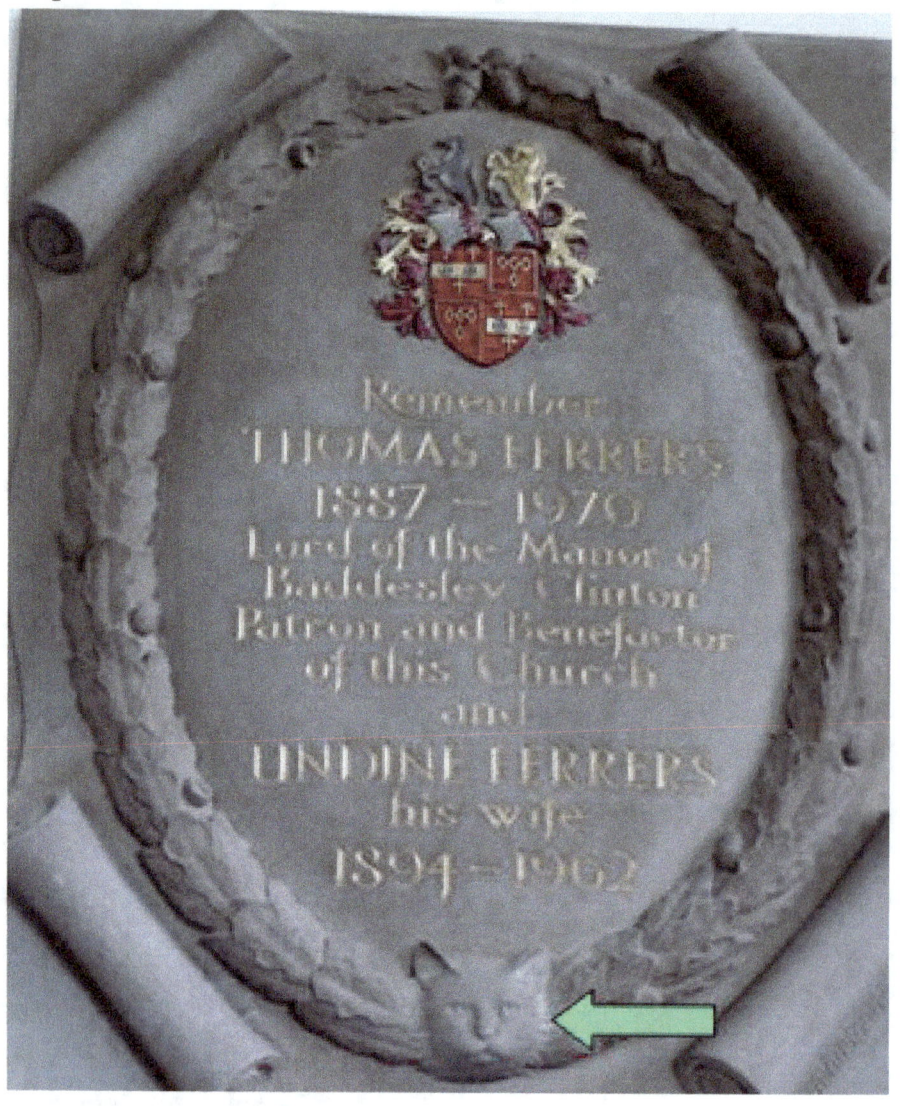

Remember
THOMAS FERRERS
1887 – 1970
Lord of the Manor of
Baddesley Clinton
Patron and Benefactor
of this Church
and
UNDINE FERRERS
his wife
1894 – 1962

Thomas Ferrers-Walker – here called Ferrers.
His cat was a constant companion.

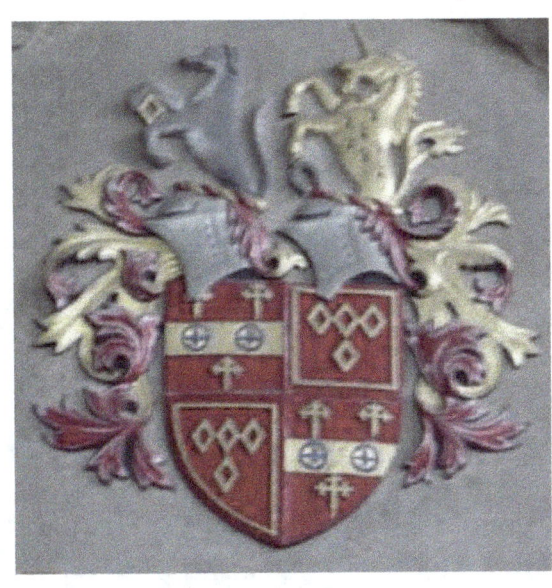

The Arms on the plaque showing Ferrers-Walker:

Qtly Walker & Ferrers.

There are numerous tapestry kneelers showing the Arms of Ferrers impaling Bird:

Photo: Chris Purvis

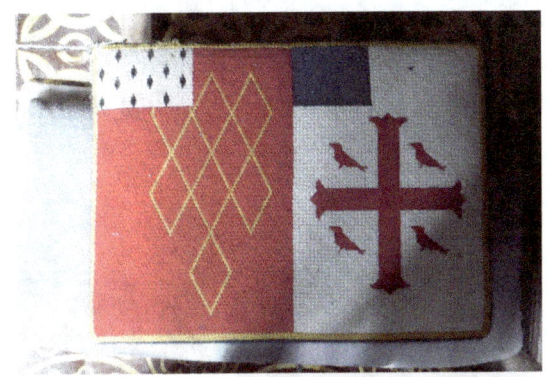

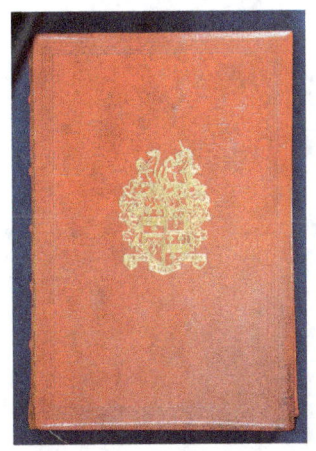

Embossed on copies of the Old & New Testaments given in Memory of Thomas & Undine « Ferrers » in 1971

Photos Chris Purvis

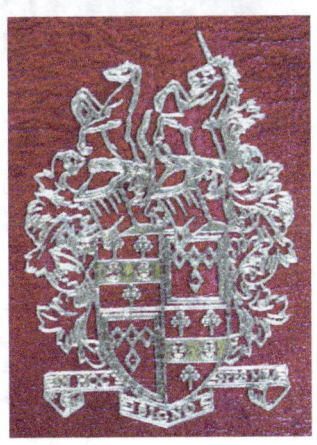

The Bishop's Chair

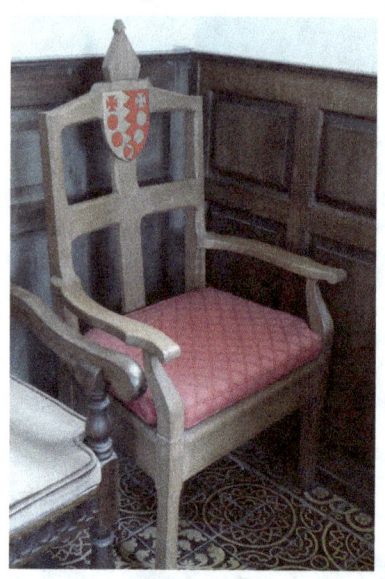 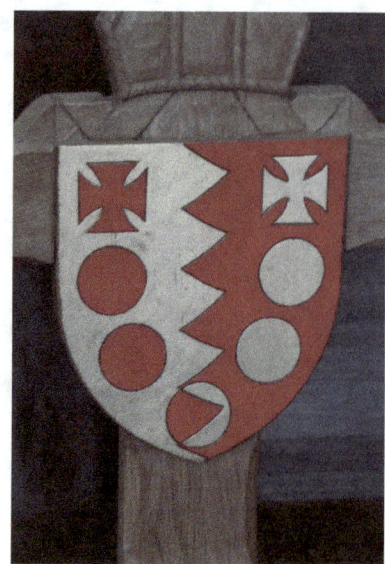

Arms of the Bishopric of Birmingham, Granted 8th March 1906, Per pale indented Arg & Gules five roundels 2,2 & 1 & in chief two crosses patée all counterchanged. Photos Chris Purvis

There is a list of the Rectors

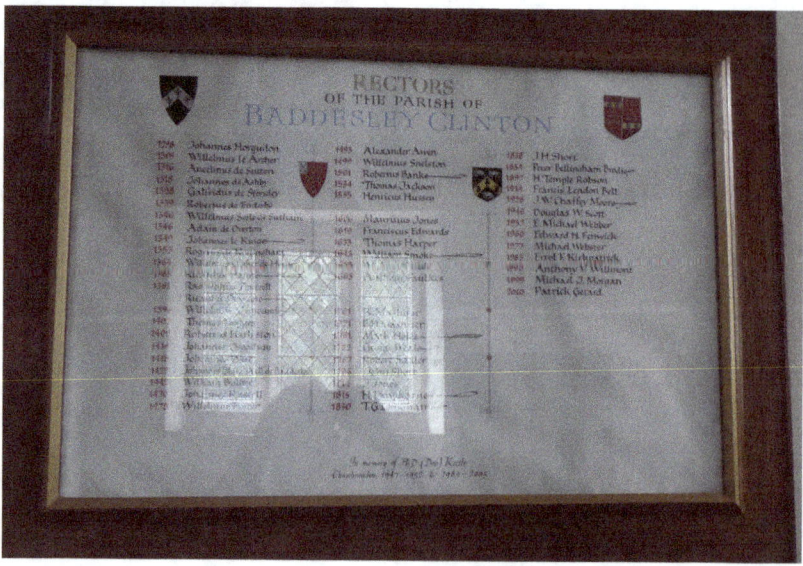

With, clockwise, the Arms of Brome, Ferrers-Walker, Iremonger & Ferrers of BC

 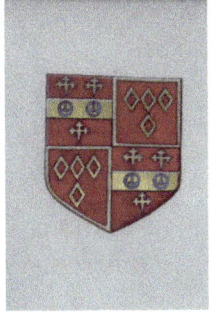 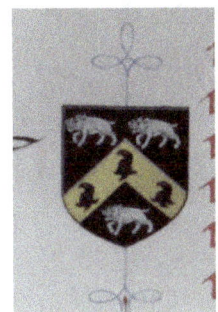 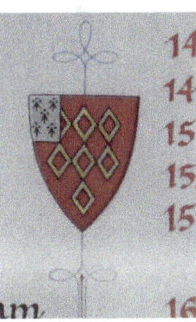

Finally, in the Graveyard

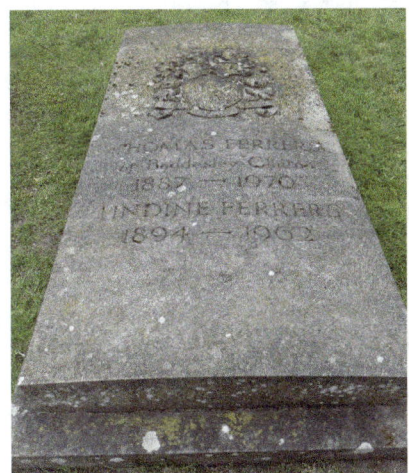

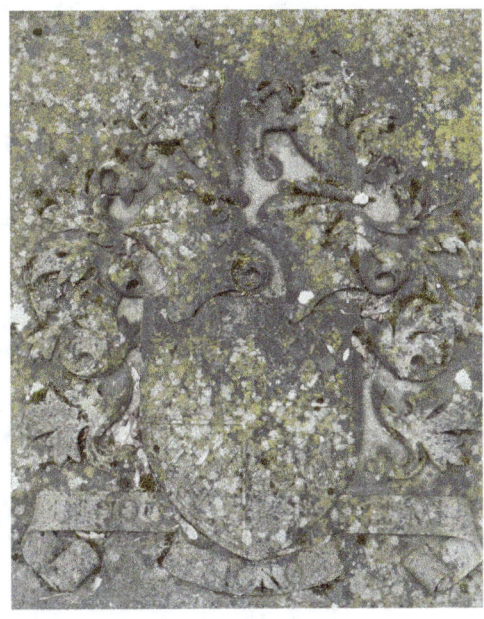

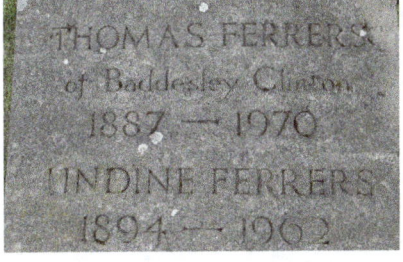

Thomas & Undine « Ferrers »

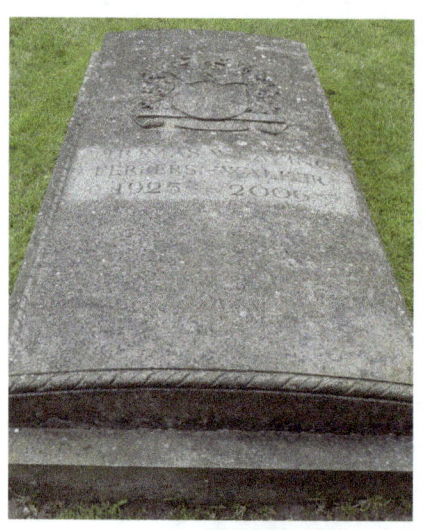

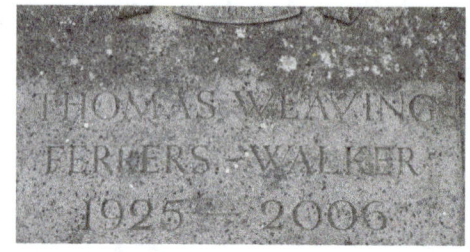

Thomas Weaving
Ferrers-Walker

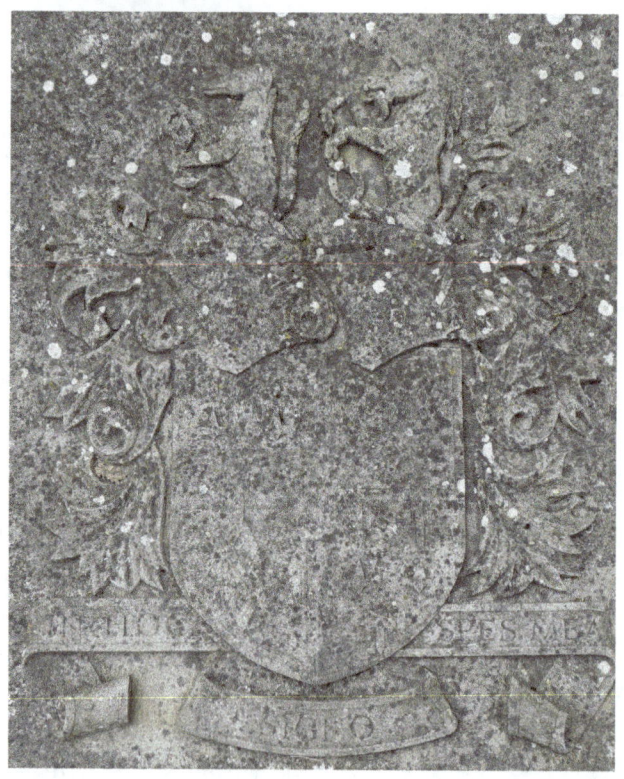

This concludes our tour of the ManorHouse and Church. I hope that you have enjoyed it?

A simple guide to the Heraldic terms used in this book.

Arms are described from the point of view of the person holding the shield - not from the point of view of the observer. Hence Right is Dexter (or left as we look at it) and left is sinister (or right, etc).

Marshalling is the arrangement of coats of arms on a shield to show various family connections.

Impalement (imp.) for a husband and wife and if the wife is an heraldic heiress - i.e. she has no brothers to carry on the line) - her husband puts her Arms on his in a small shield of pretence (i.e. he is pretending to her Arms) and their children will quarter both sets of parental Arms.

Quartering (qtly/qtrg) is when one or more families share the same blood-line and indicate this on their shield.

Is it very useful genealogically when trying to work out who married who and in which order.

The language is of Norman-French so Gules is red, Azure, blue, Vert, green and Purpure (rarely used) purple. These are known as the colours. There are two Metals, Or (yellow) and Argent (white or silver) and vaious Furs.

Then there are various divisions of the shield. These may just be single lines or more complex shapes such as chevrons and the lines may be straight or more complex. Then they may be items such as stars and animals. They are all collectively known as **charges.**

Sometimes it is all placed on something and this is called a **Compartment.**

Canting is when a charge, motto of Crest makes a pun or rebus of the name of the armiger (one who has the right to bear Arms.)

Blazon is the description of the charges put on a shield. The main divisions are described first then the charges.

A full coat of arms has a shield (without which nothing else can exist) on which sit a Helm or Crown (the shape and position of which denotes rank) and Mantling (cloth to protect the helm from heat and rain) held on by a Torse - usually six twists of coloured rope of the main colour and metal of the shield. On top of this sits the Crest (not to be confused with the Shield). There is often a Motto below (in Scotland it is placed above) and on either side and depending on rank, Supporters, which hold up the shield. The Arms may sit on a Compartment above the motto.

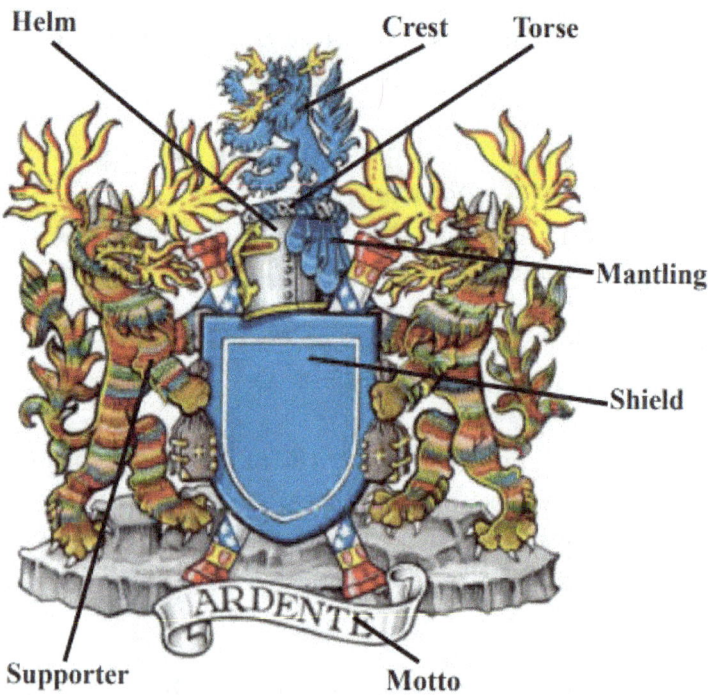

The Arms of the late Claire Boudreau
Quandam Chief Herald of Canada

Blasons, from the original booklet referred to earlier (pp. 4-5).

ANDREWES: Argent on a bend cotised Sable 3 mullets of the field. pierced of the second.

ARUNDELL: Sable 6 hirondelles Argent 3,2&1.

de AYALA: Argent 3 wolves (?dogs) Sable on a bordure Or within a bordure Or fretty Gules.

?BASSINGBORN: Gyronny of 12 Or & Azure.

BEAUCHAMP

of Hache: Vairy Azure & Argent.

BEAUFOY: Ermine on a bend Azure 3 cinquefoils Or.

BLANCHMAINS: (? Malmains) Gules 3 hands couped apaume Argent.

BLOUNT: Barry of 8 nebulee, Or & Sable.

BOTETOURT: Or a saltire engrailed Sable.

BRAOSE

of Gower: Azure 3 bars vairy Argent & Gules [shown barry of 6 vairy Argent & Gules & Azure]

BROME: Sable on a chevron Argent 3 broom sprigs vert.

de BYNTWORTH: Gules 5 lions rampant in cross Or.

CASTILE: Or a castle triple-towered.

CHATTERTON: Or a lion's head erased Azure between 3 mullets (2&1) Gules.

CHESTER: Azure 3 garbs Or.

CLIFFORD: Chequy Or & Azure a fess Gules.

COMPTON

of Northants: Sable a lion passant guardant Or between 3 esquires' helmets.

CRANLEY: Argent a fess Gules between 6 Cornish choughs Sable, legged & beaked Gules.

CROXON: Or a fess nebuly between in chief 2 cross crosslets fitchy Azure and in base a tun proper.

DERING 1: Argent a fess Azure in chief 3 torteaux.

DERING 2: Or a saltire Sable.

DEVEREUX: Argent a fess Azure in chief 3 torteaux.

DREW

of Killerton: Ermine a lion passant Gules.

ECHINGHAM: Azure fretty of 6 pieces Argent.

EDWARD THE CONFESSOR: (attributed Arms) Azure a cross moline between 5 martlets Argent.

ENGLAND: Gules 3 lions passant Or.

FERRERS -

of Baddesley Clinton: Gules 7 mascles conjoined (3,3&1) a canton of Ermine.

FERRERS (ancient): Sable 6 (3,2&1) Ferrs (horseshoes) Argent.

FERRERS

of Groby: Gules 7 mascles conjoined 3,3&1 Or

Arms of de QUINCY, via Margaret de Quincy, wife of William Ferrers.

FERRERS

of Chartley: Vairy Or & Gules.

Arms of PEVERILL via Margaret, daughter of William Peverill.

FERRERS WALKER - The Ferrers Walker quartered Coat:

Quarterly 1&4 on a fess between 3 cross crosslets fitchy Or 2 round buckles Azure

2&3 Gules 4 mascles conjoined 3&1 within an orle Or

Crests - Dexter: a demi greyhound proper holding between the paws a mascle Or

Sinister: A unicorn Erminois resting its dexter forehoof on a horseshoe proper.

Motto - "In hoc signo spec mea".

FINDERN: Argent a chevron engrailed between 3 crosses patee fitchee Sable.

FOLIOT: Gules a bend Argent.

71

FRANCE: (Modern): Azure 3 fleur-de-lys Argent.

(Ancient):Azure semee of Fleur-de-lys Argent.

FREVILL: Or a cross flory Gules.

FROGGENHALL: Sable 2 bars Or & a chief Argent.

GIFFORD: Azure 3 stirrups leathered Or.

HAMPDEN (Hamdon)

of Great Hampden: Argent a saltire Gules between 4 eaglets

displayed Azure of Great Hampden, Bucks.

HECKSTALL (Hekestall): Quarterly - Gules & Sable in the 2nd & 3rd a

fleur-de-lys Or overall a bend Argent.

IREMONGER: Sable a chevron Ermine between 3 boars

passant Or.

[Also given as: Sable on a chevron

between 3 boars passant Or as many falcons heads

erased of the field].

KEMPSON

of Ardens Grafton: Or 3 bars Vert in chief 3 molets Azure.

KNIGHTLY: Quarterly - Ermine, and paly of 5 Or & Gules a

bordure Azure.

LEOFRIC,

Earl of Mercia: (attributed Arms) Sable an eagle

displayed Or.

LOVAINE: Gules semee of billets Or a fess Argent.

LUDDEL or LUSHILL: Argent a pale fusilly Gules within a

bordure Azure bezanty.

MALMAINS: Gules 3 hands apaume couped Argent.

MANNERS,

Duke of Rutland: Or 2 bars Azure a chief quarterly of the last and Gules

- on the 1st & 4th 2 fleur-de-lys Or and

- on the 2nd & 3rd a lion of England.

MIDDLEMORE: Per chevron Argent & Sable, in chief 2

moorcocks proper.

MOLYNS: Azure a cross molines Argent

quarterpieced.

MOUNTFORD: Bendy of 10 Or & Azure

ORPEN: Per pale Azure & Or a lion rampant

counterchanged.

PEYTO: Barry of 6 per pale indented Argent & Gules

counterchanged.

PEVERILL: Vairy Or & Gules.

POPHAM: Argent on a chief Gules 2 buck's heads

caboshed Or.

POYNINGS: Barry of 6 Or & Vert on a bend Gules an

annulet Argent.

de QUINCY: Gules 7 mascles conjoined 3,3&1 Or.

R(H)ODY: Gules a cross moline voided between 4 fishes hourient

Or.

SAMBOURNE: Argent a chevron Sable between 3 mullets

pierced Sable.

SEGRAVE: Sable a lion rampant Argent crowned Or

langued & armed Gules.

SCOTLAND: Or a lion rampant between a double

tressure flory counter flory Gules.

SCUDAMORE: As Gifford but with a field Gules.

SHIRLEY: Paly of 6 Or & Azure a canton Ermine.

STRATTON: Argent on a cross Sable, 5 bezants.

SYDNEY: Or a pheon Azure.

TOWNSHEND: Azure a chevron Ermine between 3

escallops Argent.

UFFORD: Sable a cross engrailed Or.

VANNELL: Argent a chevron Vert a bordure Azure

bezanty.

VERDON: Or fretty of 6 pieces Gules [also shown as Sable].

de VERE: Quarterly - Gules & Or a molet Argent in the 1st

quarter.

de VITRY: (Unrecorded).

WHYTE

of South Wainborough: Argent a chevron Gules between 3 parrots Vert on a

border Azure 10 bezants.

WINDSORE: Gules a saltire Argent between 12 cross

crosslets Or

WOODSTOCK (Thomas):   Quarterly - FRANCE (ancient) & ENGLAND a

border Argent.

Corrections and additions. since writing the booklet:

Braose (als. Brews/Brewis Barry of six vairy Argent and Gules & Azure.

Chatterton Or a lion's head erazed Azure between 3 mullets 2&1 Gules

Compton Sable a lion passant guardant Ot between 3 esquires helmets Argent

Peyto Barry of 6 per pale indented Or and Gules all counter-changed

Vannell Argent a chevron Gules a bordure Sable bezanty.

De Vitry as Braose [als.(-) an escarbuncle (-) (1172)}

Shield 3 Upper Corridor p. 41:   **Howard** Gules a bend between 6 cross-crosslets Argent
and
Ormesby Argent a lion rampant Gules

(Roof Boss 5 p. 34: **Rafe de Badlesmere** (Kent). **Hayden** q.v.

Acknowledgements.

First and foremost I must thank the late Mr Thomas Walker (as he was then) for granting me free access to the Manor in order to complete the collection of photographs that he originally gave to me.

I appreciated the help given by the late Mr Roy McCleod for the set of ground plans and for suggesting that the Guide followed the route taken by visitors.

The details of the hatchments in the church are from Volume 1 of Peter Summers' excellent 10 volume series, *"Hatchments in Britain"*.

Finally I must thank Mr Chris. Purvis of Charlecote for his photographs which helped to fill various gaps in my collection, particularly in the Church.

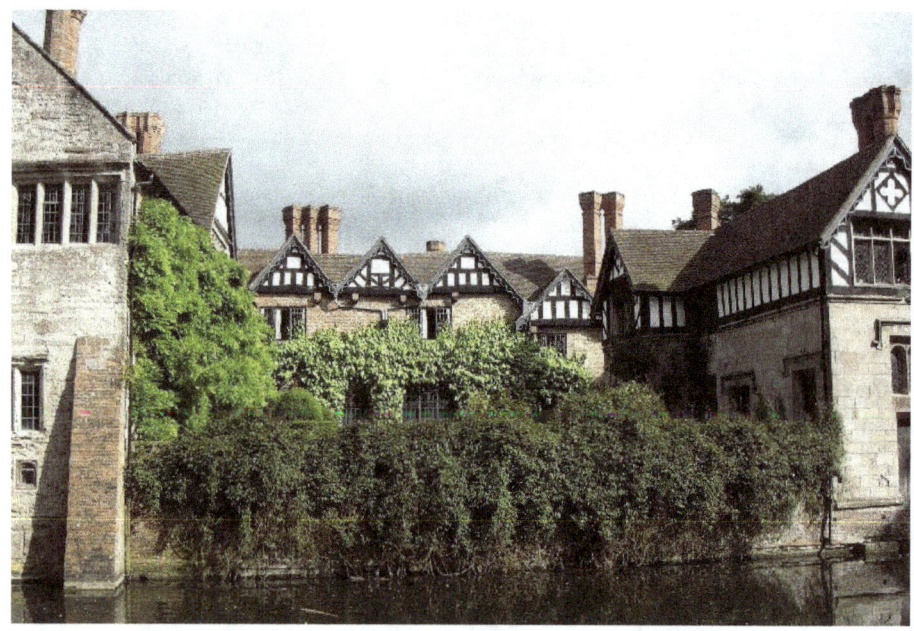

The rear view of the Manor House over the moat.

About the author.

Bernard Juby is a retired medical practitioner with a life-long interest in heraldry. He is an Honorary Fellow of the Heraldry Society and was made a Life Member of the Birmingham and Midland Society of Genealogy and Heraldry (Now Midland Ancestors) where he was in charge of heraldry for many years. He has written and edited many Church heraldry guide-books including the late Chris Smith's monumental, *"The Heraldry of Warwickshire Parish Churches"* together with numerous articles and was the Editor of, *"The Heraldry Gazette"* (the quarterly in-house magazine of the Heraldry Society) for five years.

For several decades he has been an heraldic adviser to N.A.D.F.A.S. (The National Association of Decorative & Fine Arts Societies), now called The Arts Society.

He has written the definitive study of the National Trust's, *"The Heraldry of Baddesley Clinton"* and has spent five years updating, **"Ordo Sancti Lazari"** – an over 600 page record of the coats of arms of the Knights of the Military and Hospitaller Order of St Lazarus of Jerusalem and for which he was awarded their Silver Cross of Merit.

His first book, *"The Splendour of the Heraldic Artist"* highlighted the different styles of the artists who worked mainly at or for the Officers of Arms at the College of Arms, London.

He is the founder of the facebook Group, *"Heraldic Bookplates"* which at the time of writing has over 2,500 members worldwide. His 6 volume book, *"The Splendour of the Modern Heraldic Bookplate artist"* has spawned a *Supplement* - currently in production. In July 2024 he was made a Fellow of the Birmingham and Midland Institute for designing, and steering through the College of Arms, their Grant of Armorial Bearings.

He is married, with three children, and he and his wife have retired to France where they have dual nationality. Needless to say he is deeply involved in the heraldry of the old medieval fortified border town and castle in Pouancé, Haute Anjou, where they live.